Lars Gustafsson

Forays into Swedish Poetry

Translated by Robert T. Rovinsky

University of Texas Press, Austin & London

Library of Congress Cataloging in Publication Data
Gustafsson, Lars, 1936–
    Forays into Swedish poetry.
    Translation of Strandhugg i svensk poesi.
    1. Swedish poetry—History and criticism.
I. Title.
PT9375.G813   839.7'1'009   78-5637
ISBN 0-292-72424-1
Copyright © 1978 by the University of Texas Press
All rights reserved
Printed in the United States of America
Originally published by Tidens Förlag, Stockholm, as
Strandhugg i svensk poesi, © 1977 by Lars Gustafsson.

Design by Richard Hendel
Title page illustration by Ed Lindlof

Forays into Swedish Poetry

Contents

Translator's Introduction

därför att det finns hemliga dörrar
som du inte får stänga, som ingen får stänga.
              "Arietta," 1962

because there are secret doors
which you may not close, which no one may close.
              "Arietta," 1962

At the age of only forty-two, Lars Gustafsson has already become one of the most prolific and, from the standpoint of his protean thematic concerns and ambitious artistic peregrinations through several genres, far-ranging figures on the contemporary Scandinavian literary scene. Indeed, so copious and widely discussed are the translations of his works on the Continent that he must be regarded as a significant force within the broader European context. In recognition of his considerable influence, he was invited to join West Berlin's prestigious Akademie der Künste and is now the sole Scandinavian writer in that august organization.

The Swedish author was educated at the University of Uppsala, where he earned the equivalent of an American doctorate in the field of philosophy in 1962. One can find evidence of this academic interest as well as reflections of his fascination with scientific and mathematical theory throughout his literary production, which began in 1957 with *Vägvila* (*Wayside Rest*) and includes numerous novels, short stories, plays, journalistic and editorial endeavors, essays, and books dealing with literary criticism and the history of ideas.

In his introduction to the present volume, Gustafsson notes that the analyses are built both upon his own, "naturally highly subjective view of life" and upon a more objective, structurally oriented approach which seeks to investigate the actual machinery, so to speak, of the poems. It would seem appropriate, particularly for the American reading public, which has been served but morsels from the seven volumes of his poetry—although they were quite delicious in the translations by Robin Fulton and Yvonne Sandstroem[1]—to provide a few brief examples of Gustafsson's various subjective thematic interests as voiced in his own works. As may be extrapolated from the above quote from "Arietta," which I have set as the guiding motto for this introduction, one of Gustafsson's main concerns is for what he calls, in his discussion of Södergran, "the very mysteriousness of human existence." Time and again, the poet as critic emphasizes the enigmatic, arcane aspects of life in his analyses: Strindberg's transformation of everyday reality into a "matter-of-fact mysticism" captivates Gustafsson; in Bergbo and Hansson it is the dreamlike, unreal character of the poems, the "multiplicity of meanings"; along with several others, Wecksell's poem grows into a metaphor for the impenetrability of life—in the words of Roland Barthes, "the poem understands us better than we understand the poem." And, like all the poets discussed (to paraphrase his remark in the Blomberg essay), Gustafsson uses his pen to fashion a rational context for his suffering —suffering, in his case, being synonymous with his inquisitiveness vis-à-vis life.

In an early poem, Gustafsson expressed his inability to decipher the enigmatic nature of existence:

Livet är de instängda i labyrinten:
de ser ett ljus och tror sig framme,

men glömmer att det finns ett galler.

"Upptäckter vid stillhet," 1962

Life is those closed up in the labyrinth:
they see a light and think they've arrived,

but forget that there are bars.[2]

"Discoveries in Silence," 1962

1. *Selected Poems*, trans. Robin Fulton (New York: new rivers press, 1972); *Warm Rooms and Cold*, trans. Yvonne Sandstroem (Providence: Copper Beech Press, 1975). See also "The Machines," trans. Robert T. Rovinsky, *American Review* 21 (1974): 116–125. In addition, Professor Sandstroem is presently completing a book-length critical study on Gustafsson to appear this year.
2. All translations of Gustafsson's poetry here are by Robert Rovinsky.

This frustration informs each of his subsequent collections of poetry but, by the time of the publication of *Varma rum och kalla* (*Warm Rooms and Cold*, 1972), he has transformed this feeling into a positive, if mildly sardonic, acceptance of his predicament. His "Poem on Revisionism" seems to be saying that for all his travels, physical and philosophical, and despite the recognition accorded him as a result of his literary peripatetics, he has not come an inch closer to the enigmas that confronted him from the beginning. Wisdom, in an opaque world, is unattainable. Should knowledge, in fact, be within reach, one wonders what benefit it would be for the poet/fly hurtling into the void. For all its gravity in content, however, the humorous *tone* of the poem demonstrates that Gustafsson has come to grips with his situation.

Dikten om revisionismen

Osäker fluga
instängd på ett nattsnälltåg

försöker ändå flyga
och upptäcker att det går ju utmärkt

Kommen från vagnens södra ände till den norra
redan en mycket klokare fluga

och tåget allt snabbare in i natten

Poem on Revisionism

Uncertain fly
closed up in a night express train

tries nonetheless to fly
and discovers it works very well indeed

arrived from the south end of the train at the north
already a far wiser fly

and the train all the faster into the night

In his poetry, as in a number of his essays in *Forays* (Södergran, Stagnelius), Gustafsson's vocabulary and approach bespeak a consequent, profound interest in science and technology. In its language and direction his poem of 1966, "The Machines," epitomizes the related motif of man as machine and has a direct link with the Ekelöf essay, where Gustafsson speculates on the possibility that, while we may control our own impulses, we ourselves are captives in a far greater context beyond our ken. The obvious (and most consolatory) implication of Gustafsson's machine theory, of course, is that human beings are more or less marionettes, controlled from without, and cannot be burdened with responsibility for their actions.

Maskinerna

Några av dem kom tidigt, andra sent,
och utanför den tid där den finns
är var och en av dem hemlös.

Heronskulan. Voltastapeln. Ballistan.
Blankstötsspelet i Falun. Kuriosa:
Den "pneumatiska vannan"
Una macchina per riscaldare i piedi

Maskiner urskiljer vi bara som hemlösa,
när de hör hemma i ett annat sekel.
Och då blir de tydliga, får en *betydelse*.

Vad betyder de? Ingen vet.

Stånggången: ett sätt att med två hävstänger
i fram- och återgående rörelse
överföra en kraft över stora sträckor.
Vad betyder stånggången?

DIE BERGWERKE IM HARZ ANNO 1723

Tavlan myllrar av folk. Människor,
små som flugor far upp och ned i tunnorna
och objektet "j" på tavlan, "La Grande Machine,"
vid det friska vattenfallet, driver alla linor.

Ingen har någonsin kombinerat,
vilket vore fullt möjligt,
stånggång och ångmaskin,
heronskula och voltastapel.
Möjligheten kvarstår.

Ett främmande språk, som ingen har talat.

Och noga taget:
Grammatiken själv är en maskin
som bland otaliga sekvenser
utväljer samfärdselns ramsor:
de "friska instrumenten," "födslodelarna,"
"skrien," de "kvävda viskningarna."

När orden har gått bort är grammatiken kvar,
och den är en maskin. Som betyder *vad*?
Ingen vet. Ett främmande språk.
Ett alldeles främmande språk.
Ett alldeles främmande språk.
Ett alldeles främmande språk.

Tavlan myllrar av folk. Ord,
små som flugor far upp och ned i tunnorna
och objektet "j" på tavlan, "La Grande Machine,"
vid det friska vattenfallet, driver alla linor.

The Machines

Some came early, others late,
and outside the time where it exists
each of them is homeless.

Hero's steam ball. The voltaic pile. The ballista.
Polhem's ore hoist at Falun. Curiosities:
The "pneumatic fan."
Una macchina per riscaldare i piedi.

We only perceive machines as homeless
when they belong in another century.
And then they become distinct, acquire a *meaning*.

What do they mean? No one knows.

The crankshaft: a method of transmitting
power over long distances with the aid
of two levers moving backward and forward.
What does the crankshaft device mean?

DIE BERGWERKE IM HARZ ANNO 1723

The picture swarms with people. People
small as flies ride up and down in the barrels,
and the object marked "j" in the picture, "La Grande Machine,"
by the fresh waterfall, drives all the cables.

No one has ever combined—
as would be perfectly feasible—
crankshaft and steam engine,
Hero's ball and voltaic pile.
The possibility remains.

A foreign language that no one has spoken.

And strictly speaking:
Grammar itself is a machine
which, from innumerable sequences,
selects the strings of words for communication:
the "healthy instruments," "the productive parts,"
"the cries," the "muffled whispers."

When the words have gone, grammar remains,
and it is a machine. Meaning *what*?
No one knows. A foreign language.
A completely foreign language.
A completely foreign language.
A completely foreign language.

The picture swarms with people. Words
small as flies ride up and down in the barrels,
and the object marked "j" in the picture, "La Grande Machine,"
by the fresh waterfall, drives all the cables.

Gustafsson ultimately abandoned the notion of man as automaton primarily because it could only lead to a philosophical condition of human inculpability in the face of the blatantly obvious crimes committed in the name of man. In the analysis of Key-Åberg's poem, Gustafsson very clearly dissociates himself from the viewpoint espoused in "The Machines." As a matter of fact, he wrote poems both before and after this work of 1966 which correspond to the tenor of "A Myth Is Turned Inside Out," indicating that his machine poem was probably a somewhat tentative attempt at playing philosophical *advocatus diaboli* with himself. The most well known *anti*machine poems are found in *Bröderna Wright uppsöker Kitty Hawk* (*The Wright Brothers Look for Kitty Hawk*, 1968), where, in a fantasized conversation with Baudelaire—"Anteckningar från 1860-talet" ("Notes from the 1860s") —Gustafsson brings forth a pseudoquote from the Marquis de Sade, who understood only too well man's potential for perverting the fundamentally beneficial uses for which modern technology was developed:

Ingenting inger oss bäven och lust så som vetskapen
om de tickande reläerna, elektronrören,

bruset från framtidens hetare gruvor.

Nothing inspires in us trembling and lust as does the knowledge of the ticking relays, the electron tubes,

the roar from the hotter mines of the future.

The initial expression of Gustafsson's concern with man's control and distortion of technology (rather than the reverse) came in a poem of 1963, "Calm Sequence from an Excited Film." Here, adumbrated in his vision of the dead wings, we can see an obvious connection with the crux of Key-Åberg's poem and Gustafsson's philosophical and critical appreciation of it.

Lugn sekvens ifrån en upprörd film

Det är sommar någonstans, en rikare, gammaldags sommar.
Trädens vaggande massor av löv mot brantare fasader

döljer högt uppe fönstret till ett gult skafferi
med jaktstycken, brottstycken, älskliga föremål:

korkuppdragaren där med sina två spinkiga ben
så lik en vinglande soldat av mässing i halvdagern

bland de där pilsnerflaskorna med bandet av medaljer,
alla de godhetens och brygdens äretecken som de vunnit.

Och det där redskapet med den stora gjutjärnsskruven
är en ankpress där den döda fågeln förbereds.

Så många hemligheter, så många runda njutningar
bland dessa jaktstycken, brutna och älskliga föremål

som fanns här före mig och överlämnades till lån.

Då skall dess korta vingar inte längre slå.

Calm Sequence from an Excited Film

It is summer somewhere, a richer, old-fashioned summer.
Swaying masses of leaves in the trees against steeper façades

conceal, high above, the window to a yellow pantry
with hunting gear, fragments, charming objects:

the corkscrew there with its two skinny legs
so like a staggering soldier of brass in the twilight

among these beer bottles with neckbands of medals,
all the awards for goodness and brewing that they have won.

And that instrument with the large cast-iron screw
is a duck press where the dead bird is prepared.

So many secrets, so many pure delights
among this hunting gear, broken and charming objects

which were here before me and given as a loan.

Then its wings, so short, will never beat again.

The poem "Polhem's Ore Hoist," from the 1970 collection *Kärleks-förklaring till en sefardisk dam* (*Declaration of Love to a Sephardic Lady*), spells the absolute death of the machine theme and also indicates that Gustafsson has won new confidence in man's ability to become human, so to speak, without destroying everything around him: ". . . man-as-machine has turned into man participating in the knowledge of nature."[3] The first fifteen lines of the poem are essentially identical with the spirit of "The Machines": detailed mechanical description, immense proportion, utter confidence in *the Machine*. It soon becomes obvious, however, that man is to prevail over machine, and in a very *positive* way. One is tempted to see in Christopher Polhem the figure of Lars Gustafsson, listening to the song of birds, exuding hope and trust in mankind. Since I cannot improve upon Professor Sandstroem's excellent summation of the poem and its place in Gustafsson's later production, I will include it here: "It seems as if, in *The Wright Brothers Look for Kitty Hawk*, Lars Gustafsson was on his way toward the joyous synthesis of *Declaration of Love to a Sephardic Lady*. In the 'Polhem's Ore Hoist' section, communication no longer takes place only between human marionettes. It involves man, the microcosm, with the whole macrocosm; communication is no longer mechanical but universal. Man is in nature, both in the immediate sense —the fetus in the womb, Polhem in the birch wood—and in a larger sense—the galaxies which represent the macrocosm that man both is and is part of."[4]

Berättelsen om Blankstötsspelet

Den store Polhem byggde Blankstötsspelet.
Han trodde att mekaniken var ett alfabet,

3. Sandstroem, "The Machine Theme in Some Poems by Lars Gustafsson," *Scandinavian Studies* 44, no. 2 (1972): 219.
4. Ibid.

den nya tidens skrift som skulle fylla världen
och drog genom ett vidsträckt landskap

sina *konster*, stånggångar, vändvalsverk,
knirrande trä, gnisslande järn, stockverk
i fram- och återgående rörelser som blint,
förde krafter från den ena platsen till den andra.

Av alla dessa sinnrikheter var Blankstötsspelet,
där ett väldigt hjulhus pryddes av fyra vimplar,
den allra största: från tvåhundra fots djup,
lyftes tunnorna på hakar emot dagern,

och kraften växlades igenom kyrktornshöga kugghjul.
Det var ett nytt slags värld, och genom sommarnatten,
hördes, som ett brus av stora krafter: det var människan

som några korta dagar styrde världen. Fostret,
i sitt mikrokosmos, hör de avlägsna galaxers sång,
hur radiobruset går och kommer, som blodets sus,
och när en jättestjärna störtar samman av sin egen tyngd,

och faller *inåt* och gör sitt eget ljus till mörker,
vet fostret det. Och fåglar vet sin egen riktning,
och någon mycket iskall natt vid stjärnklar himmel
kan man höra, om man snart skall dö, det jättedån,

med vilket avlägsna galaxer sakta svänger kring sin mittpunkt.

I maj står någon björkskog mycket ljus,
Christopher Polhem, i den blåa fracken, går,
och lyss till gökens sång. Det är en dag i maj.
Det är den dag då vinden vänder. Löven susar.

Av Blankstötsspelet återstår en stockhög,
sällsamma uthuggningar i en försumpad skog,
och några jättelika järnbeslag som fräts av rost.

Vimplarna fladdrade i vinden, vattnet brusade,
det jättelika hjulet bar nätt och jämnt sin egen tyngd,
och där var mera snillrikhet än trä och järn kan bära.

I Era mörka ögons djup, längst inne, har jag sett,
hur något lyste med en glans som överträffar guldets.
Inunder Era tunga ögonlock är denna hemlighet bevarad,

okända sköna med smala mycket svala händer
Ni vet det redan och Ni säger ändå inget:
Det stora hjulet brast under sin egen tyngd,

och denna *konst* i all sin sinnrikhet, sin skönhet,
drogs av vattnet, tills den brast, i fyra dagar.

Och Ni som aldrig gått bland björkar vet ändå:
Det stora Blankstötsspelet var en dröm.

Den store Polhem byggde Blankstötsspelet.

Polhem's Ore Hoist

The great Polhem built the Ore Hoist.
He thought mechanics were an alphabet,
the writing of the New Age, which would fill the world
and drew through a vast landscape

his *arts*, crankshafts, rolling mills,
creaking wood, screeching iron, stockworks,
in backward and forward movements blindly
transmitting power from one place to the other.

Of all these ingenuities the Ore Hoist,
where an enormous wheelhouse was adorned by four pennants,
was the greatest: from a depth of two hundred feet
the barrels were lifted on hooks toward the daylight,

and the power was shunted through steeple-high cogwheels.
It was a new kind of world, and through the summer night
was heard a roar as of great powers: it was man

who, for a few short days, ruled the world. The fetus
in its microcosm hears the song of distant galaxies,
how the noise of *ur*-radio waves comes and goes, like the
    murmuring of the blood,
and when a giant star collapses from its own weight,

and falls *inward*, transforming its own light to darkness,
the fetus knows. And birds know their own direction,
and on a very icy night under a starry sky
one can hear, if one is soon to die, the thunderous roar

of distant galaxies slowly swinging around their center.

In May, through a very light birch wood,
Christopher Polhem, in his blue frock coat, walks,
and listens to the cuckoo's song. It is a day in May.
It is the day the wind is turning. The leaves are sighing.

Of the Ore Hoist there now remains but a pile of wood,
peculiar clearings in a swampy forest,
and some iron mountings eaten by rust.

The pennants fluttered in the wind, the water roared,
the gigantic wheel could hardly bear its own weight,
and there was more ingenuity than wood and iron could bear.

In the depths of your dark eyes, furthest in, I have seen
something shine with a glitter surpassing gold.
Under your heavy eyelids this secret is preserved,

unknown, beautiful lady with very cool and slender hands
you already know and yet you say nothing:
The great wheel broke beneath its own weight,

and this *art* in all its ingenuity, its beauty,
was driven by the water, until it broke, for four days.

And you who've never walked among the birches still know:
The great Ore Hoist was but a dream.

The great Polhem built the Ore Hoist.

Another of Gustafsson's often explored themes, that of linguistic pessimism, is voiced in his treatment of Ekelund's "The First Spring Rain," where he restates the late nineteenth-century philosophical attitude that language has absolutely nothing to do with reality. In the Björling essay, too, it is the lacunae between the words, what is *not* being said, that bear the authority, since words, in Gustafsson's world, are at best approximative and at worst completely impotent. It is important to note that he has recently completed a lengthy philosophical treatise on linguistic pessimism, which is to be published this year: *Språk och lögn. En essä om språkfilosofisk extremism i Nittonde Århundradet (Language and Lie: An Essay on Linguistic-Philosophical Extremism in the Nineteenth Century).* A 1963 poem that illustrates perfectly—and in perfectly wry fashion—Gustafsson's point of view is "Conversation between Philosophers," for here the essentially vague and inadequate character of language is mordantly epitomized by a futile attempt at communication by two "Thinkers."

Samtal mellan filosofer

Betrakta alltså dessa skor,
gula knäppkängor, slitna till höger,
mera slitna till höger än till vänster,
betrakta för hundrade gången.

Snörhålen blankare än lädret,
ett tunt lager av damm, avskavda,

Betrakta dem noga, överväg dem!

Jag ser dem, alldeles tydligt,
ljuset faller snett, alltså eftermiddag,
så asymmetriskt de är ställda,
som för att locka ögat till sig!

Jag säger dig, du ser dem inte,
det står någon annan i vägen, han skymmer.

Men jag ser dem, de är rynkiga av steg.

Du ser ett par skor ja, ljuset är snett,
men betrakta *just dessa*! Säg vad du ser!

Det är omöjligt, det står någon annan i vägen,
just där kan jag ingenting se, just där.
Men betrakta i stället *dessa* skor,
gula knäppkängor, slitna till höger . . .

Det är omöjligt, det är något annat i vågen.

Då har du förstått mig!

Conversation between Philosophers

Observe, if you will, these shoes,
yellow button-down boots, worn on the right,
more worn on the right than the left,
observe for the hundredth time.

The lace holes shinier than the leather,
a thin layer of dust, scraped,

Observe them closely, consider them!

I see them, perfectly clearly,
the light falls obliquely (then it is afternoon),
so asymmetrically they sit there,
as if to entice the eye to themselves!

I tell you, you do not see them,
someone else stands in the way, obscuring them.

But I do see them, they are wrinkled from walking.

You see a pair of shoes, yes, the light is oblique,
but observe only *these*! Say what you see!

It is impossible, someone else stands in the way,
right there I see nothing, right there.
But observe instead *these* shoes,
yellow button-down boots, worn on the right . . .

It is impossible, there is something else in the way.

Then you have understood me!

As far as the constructional, *objective* aspects are concerned, we can see in essay after essay—Tranströmer, Stiernhielm, Ekelund, Björling, Blomberg—that Gustafsson is deeply interested in matters of form. Although he himself has written almost exclusively in free verse, it is patently clear from his analyses that he is not one who, as he notes in the Ekelund discussion, "has never learned, or even become acquainted with, any other poetic technique." Interestingly enough, as if to prove this point, during the past year Gustafsson has written a book of sonnets and has also published a number of sestinas, surely one of the most intractable of all poetic forms. Yet, while he has now evidently adopted a somewhat conservative stance with regard to form, and seems to be moving toward a more traditional, classically structured poetry, as far as the *thematic* heart of the poem and the very creative process underlying it are concerned, he is no less preoccupied with and enchanted by the prime mover of his work: the intrinsic mystery of life. And the ultimate paradox of his poetic achievement is that, as Barthes would say, his own poems understand him better than he understands them.

och dikten ler i stället för att tala,
likt en som genomskådat snabbt,

det skämt för vilket han är utsatt,
men föredrar att tiga, stillsamt le,
och tala lätt och förekommande om annat.

"Undervisning," 1962

and the poem smiles instead of speaking,
like one who has suddenly perceived

the joke of which he is the victim,
but prefers to be silent, quietly to smile,
and speak gently and courteously of other things.

"Lecture," 1962

Robert T. Rovinsky

A Partial Gustafsson Bibliography

POETRY

Ballongfararna (1962); *En förmiddag i Sverige* (1963); *En resa till jordens medelpunkt och andra dikter* (1966); *Bröderna Wright uppsöker Kitty Hawk* (1968); *Kärleksförklaring till en sefardisk dam* (1970); *Varma rum och kalla* (1972); *Sonetter* (1977).

NOVELS

Vägvila (1957); *Poeten Brumbergs sista dagar och död* (1959); *Den egentliga berättelsen om herr Arenander* (1966); *Herr Gustafsson själv* (1971); *Yllet* (1973); *Familjefesten* (1975); *Sigismund* (1976); *En biodlares död* (1978).

PLAYS

Två maktspel (1970).

ESSAYS

Utopier (1969); *Konsten att segla med drakar* (1969); *Kommentarer* (1972).

Gustafsson is a leading critic for the Swedish daily, *Expressen*, and was the managing editor of the literary-cultural journal *Bonniers Litterära Magasin* from 1962–1972.

Forays into Swedish Poetry

Introduction

For a number of years during the 1960s, I was the editor of a literary journal, and in that capacity I, of course, rejected copious amounts of poetry submitted for publication. Occasionally, it happened that some poet or another, who had been refused too many times, would become impatient and would write to ask what a poem should actually look like to be considered good poetry.

This little book contains my answer. The selection of poems that forms the basis for these analyses stretches from the earliest poetry of Sweden's Period of Great Power (1600–1718) to the present day. Enormous inner and outer distances separate the poems.

But permeating the poetry selection is one principle: no poem has been chosen unless I have been deeply convinced that it is a very good one. A small number of them (for such poems appear but rarely) belong in the category of masterpieces. Here may be counted poems such as Josef Julius Wecksell's "On Clouds You Stood" and Erik Johan Stagnelius' "To Putrefaction." Whether it is merely a difference in degree or a profound, qualitative difference that separates the masterpieces from those poems which are only very good is a controversial question which will, in all probability, be debated until the end of time.

One thing that ought to be perfectly obvious becomes plain when one sets about the task of writing a collection of poetry analyses such as these: poems are very good or are masterpieces for wholly different reasons. There are no prescriptions; an infinitude of mysterious paths leads through the primitive forests of language to the bright clearings. The ephemeral aspect of aesthetic programs and the formation of different schools emerge quite emphatically. Two poetic programs can only be mutually exclusive within one and the same poem.

If my book is able to illustrate something of the wonderful multiplicity and richness contained within the really brief history of Swedish lyric poetry, it will have fulfilled its mission.

The title is *Forays into Swedish Poetry*, and "forays" (in a strictly non-military sense) alludes to my method of approaching the poetry. In approximately the same manner as a Sunday sailor—who goes ashore at one beach after the other on a pretty summer day, has a look round, sits down for a while and observes the contours of the landscape in general (but is perhaps also struck by an interesting flower among the stones), only to weigh anchor again very soon—I have moved about quite freely, back and forth, in the great landscape of Swedish poetry. There are islands and beaches, well worth visiting, that I have not visited. On the other hand, I think I have been to a number of places which lie rather far from the most common navigable passages.

Poetry deals with something which, a bit simplistically, is usually called life. A poetry analysis worth its salt must, in one way or another, imply that the person doing the analyzing is scrutinizing life through the poem he or she holds up for consideration, in approximately the same way a photographer holds a strip of film up to the light and squints. I have not avoided showing my own, naturally highly subjective view of life in these analyses. There are scientific situations where the individual, subjective experience is an integral part of the research tools. Poetry analysis is one such situation.

For statistically oriented content analyses and frequency measurements, I have very little regard. In my view, they are based upon a false appropriation of the ideals of natural science.

But there is another form of objectivity. We can attempt to learn how something is done, that is to say, attempt to discern the objective forms in which the poem is cast. In fixed-form poetry, of course, the metrical system above all, will be important. My experiences during a brief guest appearance as Thord-Gray Professor, at the Department of Germanic Languages of the University of Texas at Austin—the only occasion in my life when I have actually instructed students in literature—tell me that it is difficult to interest modern readers of poetry in metrical feet. In some way or other, one must get them to realize that it is of such elements that the greater part of world poetry is actually comprised and that whoever does not understand the basic elements will have difficulty understanding the rest as well.

In these poetry analyses much attention is given to form.

My debts of gratitude are, naturally, enormous. Permit me to mention but a few. Professor Carl Ivar Ståhle's *Vers och språk i vasatidens och stormaktstidens svenska diktning* (*Verse and Language in the Swedish Poetry of the Wasa Period and the Period of Great Power*), which appeared in 1975, is a work that, for all time to come, must affect our view of the poetry of the Period of Great Power, not least of all because Ståhle has succeeded in unearthing such an astounding amount of previously unpublished material. Bertil Sundborg's indispensable commentary on his 1951 edition of *Wenerid* delves much deeper into the subject than may appear from a cursory glance. Another professor, Sten Malmström, has extended the boundaries for the entire metrical analysis of Swedish poetry in his 1968 *Stil och vers i svensk nittonhundratalspoesi* (*Style and Verse in Twentieth-Century Swedish Poetry*). I have also found excellent and inspiring poetry analyses by Carl Fehrman, Bengt Holmqvist, Sven Lindner, and Sven Linnér.

For the present English edition, I owe further thanks to Professor Magnus von Platen of Umeå University in Sweden, the eminent expert on earlier Swedish poetry, who was of great assistance in establishing definitive text versions for some of the older poems.

This edition, particularly the English versions of the poems, is the result of very close cooperation between the translator, Professor Robert T. Rovinsky, and myself. Thanks are due, in this connection, to the Swedish Institute for Cultural Relations, which helped make this effort possible, and to the University of Texas at Austin, which, generous as always, placed its facilities at the disposal of this Swedish guest.

In his entertaining America novel of 1974, *Orfeus i överjorden* (*Orpheus in Paradise*), Christian Stannow describes a scene from the University of Texas at Austin. Outside, it is a quivering 95 degrees. The students—some are blacks, some Mexican Americans, some wear the long, tapering Texas mustache—listen as a lazy breeze wafts through the mighty trees outside the window. The professor, Bob T. Newzeuski, is writing on the blackboard, and the students are copying endlessly:

> O mina barn! Ej hundra offertjurars blod,
> Trollformler och mystèrer, helga vågors bad
> Borttvätta själens smitta. Lydnad blott för den

Som öppnar och som sluter Orki kopparport,
Stavbärarn Hermes, Majas vingbeklädda son.[1]

I have had the privilege of becoming acquainted with several of these heroic Scandinavianists in foreign countries who, year after year, write lines from Stagnelius' "Backanterna" ("The Bacchantes") on blackboards, accompanied by the soughing of foreign trees. They have taught me something about the love of Swedish poetry which I did not understand before I met them, and I am taking the liberty of mentioning those who have been my strongest sources of inspiration: Professor Torborg Lundell, University of California; Professor Otto Oberholzer, University of Kiel, Germany; Professor John Weinstock, University of Texas; and, naturally, Professor Robert T. Rovinsky, University of Texas.

Lars Gustafsson

1. O my children! Not even the blood from a hundred sacrificial steers,
   Incantations and mysteries, the holy water's bath
   Can wash away the spirit's pest. Nothing but obedience to him,
   Who opens and closes the copper gates of Orcus,
   Staff-bearing Hermes, Maia's wingèd son.

Skogekär Bergbo

Wenerid: Tionde sonetten

Så syntes mig hon tog min hatt i sina händer
och gick så därmed ut; dessmillan sökte jag.
Det såg hon, ropa mig, fick hatten, sade: tag!
Och så milt leende sig saktlig från mig vänder.

Ett frihets tecken är en hatt. Ty när det händer
att trälar frihet givs, så är det gammal lag
att giv' en hatt. Så tror jag ock hon få behag
omsider frälsa mig och mig min frihet sänder.

Men hurudan frihet? Att jag ej älskar mera?
Få det jag älskat har? Det förra kan ej ske,
det är otrolig ting så vidt jag än kan se.

Dock tyckte mig jag fick sist gunstetecken flera
och tror ännu som förr: så hård är ingen skön,
som blötes ej av en rätt älskars trägne bön.

omkring 1650

Wenerid: Tenth Sonnet

It seemed to me she took my hat into her hands
and left with it; while search did I both far and near.
And seeing this, she took the hat and called, said: Here!
And then, so mildly smiling, slowly from me wends.

A sign of freedom is a hat. Old law commands
that slaves be given such, their liberty to cheer.
That she would cherish such a law to me seems clear,
For there, to set me free, so graciously she stands.

But freedom of what sort? That I may love no more?
To win the one I've loved? The former cannot be,
it is not to believe as far as I can see.

But many signs of favor last to me she bore,
and I do still believe: no beauty is so hard,
cannot be softened by a suitor's bold regard.

circa 1650

Skogekär Bergbo's Dream

In the year 1680, the sonnet collection *Wenerid För mehr än trettio åhr skrifwin (Wenerid, Written More than Thirty Years Ago)* was published. One of the great debates in Swedish literary research centers about who the author actually was. The author whose name appeared on the front fly-leaf of this and of two other small books of poetry from 1658 and 1682 was Skogekär Bergbo.

The theories have varied. For quite some time, the diplomat Schering Rosenhane was the favorite. More recent research, represented, for instance, by Bertil Sundborg, has advanced interesting arguments in support of the theory that the author was President Gustaf Rosenhane, brother of the brilliant Schering. Equally unresolved is the question of who the lovely woman is whom Skogekär Bergbo celebrates in song. Queen Christina's beautiful and much-fêted lady-in-waiting, Ebba Sparre, is one of the candidates proposed.

But let us allow the identity of Skogekär Bergbo to remain an open question.

The tenth sonnet in *Wenerid* will remain just as captivating even if we never learn who wrote it or for which woman it was written. One of the reasons for this is, quite simply, that it is a description of a dream.

Dream depictions in older Swedish poetry are often stylized, arranged specifically to suit polemical, chivalrous, or other lawful purposes. The dream as dream, not as morality or prophecy or educative fable, belongs strictly to lyrical modernism.

But, in Skogekär Bergbo's sonnet, there is a genuine interest in the dream itself, in its manifold meanings, in the various possibilities of interpretation. And does not the poem itself possess something of the dream's *gliding*, uncertain character, which is only given emphasis by the sonnet form?

The sonnets in *Wenerid* follow the same rhyme scheme as the classical Italian sonnet (a-b-b-a, a-b-b-a), not the Shakespearean form, which later came to be the most common interlacing rhyme pattern in Swedish sonnets (a-b-a-b, a-b-a-b). The Renaissance ideal for the sonnet also stipulated that the octave, the first two groups of four lines each, should be contradicted by the sestet, the two groups of six lines, three lines in each group, which conclude the poem.

Literary historians often describe Skogekär Bergbo's sonnets as slightly awkward, embryonic attempts to transfer this prestigious Mediterranean form to the bare-boned Swedish of the seventeenth century.

I think they are mistaken. Bergbo's dream poem is a consummate specimen of the sonnet genre. The number of syllables varies somewhat freely, but this can also occur in Petrarch. And notice how exquisitely the poet places the paradox in the first of the sestet's stanzas! Is it that she is leaving him, or that she is coming to him, that constitutes the freedom?

That "blötes," in the poem's final line, should not have its modern meaning, "vätes" ("is made wet"); rather, the meaning "uppmjukas" ("is softened"), is easily understood by the modern reader. "Blöt," in fact, still means "soft" in Norwegian. Otherwise, the poem presents hardly a single linguistic problem, although three hundred years will soon have passed since it was published.

"And then, so mildly smiling, slowly from me wends" seems to me to be the finest line in the poem. It truly has something of the gentle inexorability of a dream scene. This is how the people we love or are dependent upon often appear in our dreams; kindly, but resolutely, they turn away, as if captured by a greater context, which we are unable to view, or driven by a stronger impelling force. There is a marvelous finesse in Wenerid's shy movement in the poem, but there is also a multiplicity of meanings.

Perhaps, deep down, it was this that the unknown poet wanted: for her to turn away, for him to be permitted to be alone with his feelings of love, undisturbed by the capricious reality always implicit within a woman loved.

Josef Julius Wecksell

På moln stod du

På moln stod du! Jord voro dina fötter och din
      tanke räckte upp till Gud!
Dina ögon slog du upp och var atom i ditt sinne
      var en skapelse.
Du sträckte ut din hand och sade: vad är du?
      och det var luft.
Och din ande gick ut och du såg stjärnor och
      solar fara förbi som moln.
Och du ropade: himmelen stod under Guds
      fötter.
Och därovan var mörker dit ingen hann och du
      visste din moders liv och du önskade
      en kvinna.
Och en poppel stod grön i det innersta av ditt öga
och din storhet försvann och du låg som en tår
på din egen fot i din egen glans
och molnet var försvunnet.

                          1860-talet

On Clouds You Stood

On clouds you stood! Earth were your feet and your
        thought reached up to God!
You opened your eyes and every atom in your mind
        was a creation.
You stretched out your hand and said: what are you?
        and it was air.
And your spirit was projected and you saw stars and
        suns passing by like clouds.
And you cried out: the sky was standing under God's
        feet.
And above there was darkness which none could reach and you
        knew your mother's womb and you desired
        a woman.
And a poplar stood green in the innermost of your eye
and your greatness vanished and you lay like a tear
on your own foot in your own splendor
and the clouds had vanished.

                    1860s

A Poplar Stood Green in Your Eye

There exist certain poems for which any attempt at analysis will strike one as sheer insolence. It is in these rare masterpieces that it is obvious to us, from the very first moment, that—to borrow an expression from the French critic, Roland Barthes—the poem understands us better than we understand the poem.

It is remarkable that one of the greatest, most indestructible masterpieces in the history of Swedish lyric poetry should have been written by a young, at that time already mentally disturbed, Åbo student during the second half of the nineteenth century, some time after 1863—at a time, that is to say, when Swedish lyric poetry in general was reaching one of the lowest ebbs in its history.

In Åbo, in the shadow of the cathedral, directly behind the library, we can still meet Josef Julius Wecksell today, in the form of Yrjö Liipola's bronze statue. A beautiful, pensive youth, clad in the student tailcoat of his time. He is gazing down at the ground, as if he had caught sight of something. With both hands reaching ever so slightly backward, he is supporting himself against the foundation, as if what he was looking at made him dizzy and as if he wanted to make sure there was still solid ground behind him. It is the image of a man who, while taking a peaceful stroll, suddenly sees an abyss opening up in front of him.

It is an excellent portrait. Wecksell was born in 1838, the son of a craftsman who had emigrated to Finland from Sweden. A precocious college poet, he was already being praised as a great writer in the Finland-Swedish camp at the age of twenty-two, when his *Valda ungdomsdikter* (*Selected Juvenile Poems*) appeared. Two years later, in 1862, his tragedy, *Daniel Hjort*, had its first performance. It is the first realistic tragedy in Swedish literature, and Karin Allardt Ekelund has called it "one of the most powerful dramas in Swedish literature before Strindberg, with a pioneering, democratic view of the Finnish people."

And then it all ended. Wecksell was struck by the same fate as so many other suddenly flaring, extremely talented young poets: after the initial explosion of ecstatically colored artistic mastery, an extinguishing, a path leading into drabness. But Wecksell's destiny was even crueler than that which hit, for example, Rimbaud. On the twenth-eighth of September 1865, the gates of Lappviken's insane asylum closed behind him. He lived there, mute, enclosed in a world about which we can know nothing, for the horribly protracted period of time all the way up to 1902.

There are good reasons to assume that "On Clouds You Stood" stems from the period between 1863 and 1865.

What is it about? The breakdown itself, the dissolution of reality, the step from an infinitely heightened sense of self-esteem to the tremendous smallness of an extinguished sensitivity to life? And everything in brilliant abbreviation: all in all, it gives the impression of having occurred with frightening speed.

There is a condition, brought about by fever or just before dreaming, in which even the more commonplace psyches *we* possess are able to experience something which remotely resembles this. Your own body suddenly feels terribly large, like a cathedral or an entire continent, and at the same time you think of yourself as a tiny circular atom somewhere in your own body.

Perhaps it is an interference phenomenon, a disturbance that arises between two types of brain waves—what do I know?—but it provides a kind of entrance into the poem.

But transforming the poem into a case history of an abnormal phenomenon would be tantamount to diminishing it. "On Clouds You Stood" contains a truth which is much more objective and much more universal.

"Your thought reached up to God," the poet says, but only a few lines later he himself is literally God. Stars and suns slip past. According to Sigmund Freud, there is a condition in the development of the very smallest child when it still considers itself to be omnipotent. It has not yet discovered the disappointments which, for all of us, comprise the limitations of tangible existence. In a few extreme personalities, a vestige of this childish condition may still be present. All the more terrible the disappointment, then, when this ambition of the subconscious is thwarted. It is possible to trace a profoundly unhappy love affair behind Wecksell's final years as a poet.

There can be found, paradoxically enough, a quality of just this kind of deep childishness in this extremely sophisticated poem. It even says, "you / knew your mother's womb and you desired / a woman."

Actually, the reply to this poem can be found in Swedish literary history, in the wise and, at the same time, kindred spirit of Erik Johan Stagnelius:

> . . . The laws are two that rule
> this life, Power to desire
> is the first. Constraint to renounce
> the second. Ennoble into liberty
> this constraint . . .[1]

> "The Mystery of Sighs," 1821

But what is the meaning of this fantastic line: "And a poplar stood green in the innermost of your eye"?

Like a strange green torch, as the final color in Wecksell's soon-to-be black and white world, this poplar blazes toward us after more than a century.

---

1. . . . Tvenne lagar styra
   detta liv. Förmågan att begära
   är den första. Tvånget att försaka

   är den andra. Adla du till frihet
   detta tvång . . .
   "Suckarnes Mystèr," 1821

August Strindberg

Gatubilder III

Mörk är bäcken, mörkt är huset—
mörkast dock dess källarvåning—
underjordisk, inga gluggar—
källarhalsen är båd' dörr och fönster—
och därnere längst i mörkret
syns en dynamo som surrar,
så det gnistrar omkring hjulen:
svart och hemsk, i det fördolda
mal han ljus åt hela trakten.

Ordalek och småkonst, 1902

Street Scenes III

Dark is the hill, dark the house—
but darkest is its cellar—
subterranean, windowless—
the staircase serves as door and window—
and down there deepest in the darkness
stands a humming dynamo,
sparks flying around its wheels:
black and horrifying, hidden,
it grinds light for the entire neighborhood.

Word Play and Minor Art, 1902

Strindberg and His Generator

This extraordinary poem is the third in a cycle by Strindberg called "Street Scenes" which forms part of his *Word Play and Minor Art* from 1902.

On the surface, it is a naturalistic poem, written in deliberate protest against the poetic idealism which, for Strindberg, was embodied initially by the Signature Poets, who, during his youth, distributed literary academy prizes among themselves and loved to represent themselves as unassuming sparrows around the table of Poetry.[1] This poetic approach was then later propounded by Heidenstam and his school.[2] On Easter Day 1901, Strindberg writes, in a rather desperate letter to his third wife, Harriet Bosse:

> Might it be possible that my sufferings could be turned into joy for others? Well, let me suffer then! I think of that black electricity machine, placed down in that cellar on Gref Magnigatan, black and terrifying. It sits there, dark in the darkness, and grinds light for the whole block![3]

It is possible that this generator was situated in the cellar of Gref Magnigatan 12, where Harriet Bosse had an apartment after her divorce from Strindberg, or in some adjacent house. Perhaps there is an expert on Stockholm and its first power generators who might even be able to locate it?

There is no doubt that the generator is described in naturalistic fashion: even the imperfect contactors of the time, the so-called car-

1. This group of nine young poets at the University of Uppsala was dedicated to a return to simplicity in poetry. Toward this end, they banded together in the 1860s to form the Namnlösa Sällskapet (The Nameless Society) and became known as the Signature Poets because of their collaborative publication, *Sånger och berättelser av nio signaturer* (*Songs and Tales of Nine Signatures*, 1863). Of the nine, only one, Carl Snoilsky (1841–1903), achieved subsequent fame as a poet.
2. Verner von Heidenstam (1859–1940).
3. Torsten Eklund, ed., *August Strindbergs brev*, vol. 14 (Stockholm: Bonniers förlag, 1974), p. 62.

bon brushes, which sparked and crackled when picking up the induced direct current, can be found in the poem. Of course, it is naturalism to write about an electric generator, a novel and frightening element in the composition of the city.

But, as is often the case in the Strindberg who has the Inferno crisis behind him, the realistic image is used to create an inner reality. There arises a kind of matter-of-fact mysticism—a *dry* mysticism, if you will—of the same type as is found in *Ett Drömspel* (*A Dream Play*, 1901), where a pantry door with a clover-shaped air hole is made to represent the door to a metaphysical reality.

This is part of a Swedish tradition of matter-of-fact directness. It is present in both Linnaeus and Swedenborg and continues in Pär Lagerkvist, who, in *Det eviga leendet* (*The Eternal Smile*, 1920), allows God to saw wood in the kingdom of the dead, and in Gunnar Ekelöf, with his poem on the old cargo-master and his fantasized ideal gastronomical menu.[4]

"Street Scenes" appeared in 1902, that is, only a few years before Freud's *Drei Abhandlungen zur Sexualtheorie* (1910). If it had been the other way around, of course, one would have said that Strindberg's poem was profoundly influenced by Freudianism. Where could we find a better metaphor for Freud's subconscious than this generator, which, like the libido, the elemental human drive, stands there, black and terrible, humming in the darkness, yet still producing light for the entire area? After all, it is through a sublimated sexual urge that works of art are created. According to Freud.

In addition, the remarkable line in the poem, where Strindberg speaks about the actual construction of the room—"the staircase serves as door and window"—is well worth noting.

It is, of course, a human *womb* that is being described, the dark room which has only one connection with the outside world! And which is also a life-giving room.

It often leads only to confusion, Thomas Mann says, to delve too deeply into the inner circumstances surrounding a work of art, into its personal background. Strindberg's poem has a self-portraying

4. *Sent på jorden* (1932).

quality which certainly should not be underestimated. From out of a dark and painful subconscious flows the power which lights the lamps of art:

> black and horrifying, hidden,
> it grinds light for the entire neighborhood.

The surprising Freudian quality of the poem actually should not be so surprising at all. The ideas could be found in Strindberg's intellectual environment. Hartmann's *Philosophie des Unbewussten* had been in existence for a good many decades when the poem was being written. The entire view of the relationship between art and the subconscious, which is found in Freud, was in the air in the intellectual Europe of the turn of the century.

But it is possible to reach even deeper strata in the analysis of this work. It possesses the kind of inexhaustibility characteristic of truly significant poetry.

There are, for example, bridges—perhaps subterranean connections would be better—between Strindberg's poem and what would become literary modernism approximately thirty years later (considerably delayed, according to European standards).

Strindberg's generator stands there and *grinds* light for the entire area; it is a new kind of mill in a Stockholm which has begun to change, where the old mills are beginning to disappear along with the gas lights.

Thirty years later, in 1932, a lamp *spins* light in another great Swedish poem, namely, in the introduction to Gunnar Ekelöf's *Sent på jorden (Late upon the Earth)*:

> The flowers lean
>   toward the light and the lamp
>   spins light[5]

5. blommorna lutar sig
       mot natten och lampan
   spinner ljus

Mills grind and spinning wheels spin. Old, ancient verbs now assuming new roles. The world is being changed, conceptual horizons expanded. The old words are given new uses. "Light it," my parents still say when referring to an electric lamp. But my children say, "Turn it on." What exists in the crannies between that which is still nameless and the old names?

It is through just this kind of experiencing of linguistic cracks that what we call literary modernism receives much of its power. If the August Strindberg who wrote *A Dream Play* and *Word Play and Minor Art* had been permitted to exert a greater influence on Swedish lyric poetry at the turn of the century, perhaps we would have had a literary modernism in Sweden at the same time as in France.

Bertil Malmberg

Afton

In under den tysta, blå skuggan
församla sig popplarna.

Men bortom marterpålarna, 1948

Evening

Under the silent, blue shadow
the poplar trees gather.

But Beyond the Stakes of Torture, 1948

Evening with Thunder

Bertil Malmberg's short poem, "Evening," could first be read in his collection *But Beyond the Stakes of Torture* in 1948. Today, Malmberg is forgotten by the general public. His conservatism, a certain theatrical quality in his personality, which was complemented by a rhetorical quality in some of his poetry, has obscured the fact that he was one of the major poets of the first half of the century.

"Evening," as far as I can see, is one of the most brilliant short poems in the Swedish language. Each word has the same urgent necessity, the same obviousness as the brushstrokes in a fine old Japanese drawing—or, if you will, as the thematic movements in Bach's "Goldberg Variations," where the end of every phrase forms the beginning of the next one.

The poem is a painting.

It is, of course, vital for the entire effect, that the poem turns nature around. It is not the blue shadow of evening that sweeps in over the landscape; rather, it is the landscape that is sucked in toward the shadow, which itself is standing still. This creates a paradoxical mood, which at the same time becomes so self-evident that the reader need not even intellectually understand the strange element in order to experience it.

Bertil Malmberg published an analysis of the poem in his autobiography, *Förklädda memoarer* (*Disguised Memoirs*), in 1956. There he says the following:

> It is the poplars that glide or drive toward the blackness, whereas the darkness is static and remains in its place. Everything moves toward the passively waiting ineluctability. The artistic impression, then, is that of a landscape in motion. But the shadow, where it ends up, is *silent* and *blue*; it provides an apprehension of the peace of eternity. And the poplars, although compelled by destiny, *gather together* nonetheless—this allows us to experience something of a clandestine free will in that which is fated, inevitable. Obliteration, where all life perishes or is absorbed, is at the same time the maternal.

As is evident, Malmberg mentions only indirectly the enormously

strong death wish which is, in fact, the most conspicuous characteristic of the entire poem. It is only indirectly as well that he mentions
the equally strong passivity in the attitude of the entire poem. Here
there is no room for plots and slogans. What happens, happens ir-
retrievably.

There is a quality of *childishness* in the poem which requires some
time to comprehend. The poplars that glide beneath the silent, blue
shadow, the entire tenor of hopelessness, of "that's how it has to be,"
remind me of the thunder-filled summers of my childhood—the entire feeling of restlessness that descends upon one and then changes
to resignation at the moment the first drops of water begin to fall.
The terror in this poem is a childish terror; childish, too, is its trust
in what has to be. It is no accident that Malmberg, in his own analysis, speaks of maternity.

How swift, actually, is the movement in the poem?

It may be more rapid than one believes at first. The entire concept
of a landscape in motion is present everywhere in the painting of
expressionism, which was so significant for Bertil Malmberg's artistic
development. We have seen it before: Edvard Munch's *The Scream* is,
naturally, the most obvious image with which to associate this. The
difference consists in the fact that Malmberg's poem is much more
submissive.

But perhaps the slowness is only apparent. Perhaps it is the onset
of a storm we are witnessing.

To allow oneself to be swept along by Malmberg's ingenious little
poem is to be drawn into passivity—into childishness, if you will.
There is something of the twelve-year-old child's endless melancholy
behind the poem's German expressionistic mask (poplars—not
birches), an almost biological conservatism, a feeling which occasionally, not always, has something to do with political conservatism,
inasmuch as it represents the world as something we cannot change
to any particularly great extent, something we can hardly even reach.

I do not consider it at all unsound or foolish to spend some time
with this poem. These moods are present, under every conceivable
circumstance, in ourselves. They are essentially an important part of
us, like fatigue, like melancholy, like an "oh, let whatever happens
happen!"

Tomas Tranströmer

Storm

Plötsligt möter vandraren här den gamla
jätteeken, lik en förstenad älg med
milsvid krona framför septemberhavets
        svartgröna fästning

Nordlig storm. Det är i den tid när rönnbärs-
klasar mognar. Vaken i mörket hör man
stjärnbilderna stampa i sina spiltor
        högt över trädet.

17 dikter, 1954

Storm

Suddenly, here, the wanderer meets the ancient
giant oak tree, like a petrified moose with
mile-wide crown, before the September seascape's
        nightly green fortress

Northerly storm. It is the time when rowanberry
clusters ripen. Awake, one hears in the darkness
constellations stamping in their stables
        high over oak tree.

17 Poems, 1954

Classical Dance Rhythms on Autumnal Swedish Skerries

Tomas Tranströmer's "Storm" first appeared in his debut collection, *17 Poems*, published in 1954. For all its apparent simplicity, it bears the imprint of a master-hand. It takes a little while before one discovers this.

Let us see how it is made!

The poem consists of two stanzas, each of which has three long lines and a short concluding line, in which the rhythm seems to run in a direction counter to that of the longer lines. The long lines consist of the following rhythmic system: first, there are two trochees—that is to say, disyllabic metrical feet with falling rhythm (dá-dĭt, dá-dĭt)—then, there is a complicated metrical foot whose rhythm is the same as the word AÚTŎMŎBÍLE. In classical Greek poetics, this is called choryamb, or "limping iamb." Finally, the line is concluded with a foot the experts usually call an additional metron. It sounds approximately like this: dĭ-dá-dă. The short fourth line consists of a dactyl and a trochee: dá-dĭ-dĭ, dá-dĭt. It is the same rhythmic pattern which concludes the line in a classical hexameter (wonderful bits of cake, both lighter and *darker in color*). This pattern is called the Adonic in classical poetics.

Together, the intricate interweaving of rhythms moving back and forth against each other, and seemingly contradicting one another (something like a folk dance troupe executing complicated steps), forms the classical poetic measure of antiquity, which is commonly called the Sapphic stanza. Horace is the great master of this form.

Tomas Tranströmer uses it, with marvelous dexterity, in many places in *17 Poems*. It is, in other words, fixed-form but unrhymed poetry. Classical Latin poetry is being made to lend its form to a piece of Swedish poetry from the 1950s. Austere dance rhythms from antiquity—on austere, autumnal skerry cliffs. The September sea pounding in this poem reaches deep down into its rhythms, providing both gravity and rapid movement.

"Storm" is replete with fascinating parallels. In the first stanza, the poet exhibits an enormously original touch, comparing an ancient, gigantic tree to a petrified moose with a mile-wide crown.

The moose, that creature so loved by Swedish cartoonists—perhaps because it always seems so alien to us, so closed up in its own world—waxes into something great and solemn, an animal out of a fable. Petrified, the moose becomes frightening; an atmosphere of primeval times, of prehistoric dread, surrounds this image.

"It is the time when rowanberry clusters ripen" is actually a very solemn, almost ritualistic way of saying that it is early autumn.

There is an amusing connection between this intonation and the nature-oriented, very bourgeois poetry of the first decades of the twentieth century, where the most prominent names are Anders Österling and Gunnar Mascoll Silfverstolpe. There is a poem by Silfverstolpe which speaks about the conclusion of a summer vacation:

> It was the time our pockets started bulging
> from bruise-edged fruit with rain-soaked, muddy skin.[1]
> "End of Summer Vacation," 1926

In Tranströmer's first stanza, there is something living and moving which becomes petrified: the moose. In the second stanza, something fixed and immobile—the constellations—become living, restless horses, who stamp in their stables high above the tree.

Tranströmer loves this paradox: what appears to be still is actually in violent motion; what seems to be moving is, in reality, standing stock-still. In another part of *17 Poems*, one can find "Stenarnas pingst" ("The Pentecost of the Stones").

There is a tremendous inner agitation in Tranströmer's poetry, a restrained impatience. And, like the Christian poet he is, he always transforms this restrained, closed-in life in nature into a kind of symbol. A symbol for what? For the fact that time will eventually cease? That God does exist? That nature, too, is waiting for a resurrection?

It is difficult to say. Unlike the lachrymose, sentimental Christian poetry that appeared at the close of the 1960s, Tranströmer's is always dry, objective, reserved. It retains its enigma.

---

1. Det var den tid då våra fickor spändes
   av kantstött frukt med regnvåt lera på.
      "Slut på sommarlovet," 1926

Gunnar Ekelöf

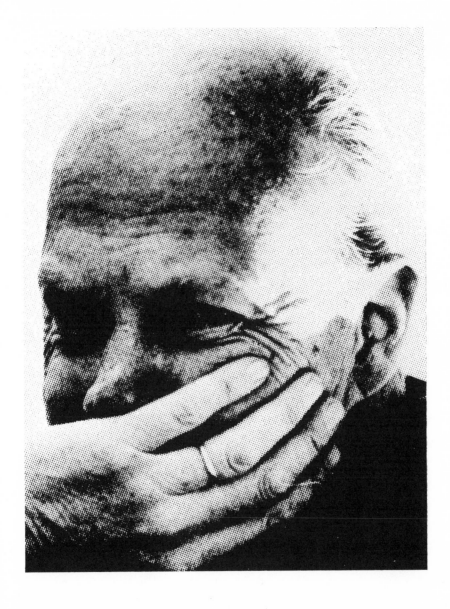

En värld är varje människa

En värld är varje människa, befolkad
av blinda varelser i dunkelt uppror
mot jaget konungen som härskar över dem.
I varje själ är tusen själar fångna,
i varje värld är tusen världar dolda
och dessa blinda, dessa undre världar
är verkliga och levande, fast ofullgångna,
så sant som jag är verklig. Och vi konungar
och furstar av de tusen möjliga inom oss
är själva undersåtar, fångna själva
i någon större varelse, vars jag och väsen
vi lika litet fattar som vår överman
sin överman. Av deras död och kärlek
har våra egna känslor fått en färgton.

Som när en väldig ångare passerar
långt ute, under horisonten, där den ligger
så aftonblank.—Och vi vet inte om den
förrän en svallvåg når till oss på stranden,
först en, så ännu en och många flera
som slår och brusar till dess allt har blivit
som förut.—Allt är ändå annorlunda.

Så grips vi skuggor av en sällsam oro
när något säger oss att folk har färdats,
att några av de möjliga befriats.

Färjesång, 1941

Every Human Is a World

Every human is a world, populated
by blind beings in dark revolt
against the ego, the king who rules over them.
In every soul a thousand souls are captive,
in every world a thousand worlds are hidden
and these blind, these lower worlds
are real and living, though premature,
as truly as I am real. And we kings
and princes of the thousand possible within us
are subjects ourselves, captive ourselves
in some greater being, whose ego and essence
we comprehend as little as our superior
his superior. From their death and love
our own feelings have received a coloring.

As when a great steamer passes by
far out, below the horizon, where it lies
so evening-smooth.—And we know nothing of it
until a swell reaches us here on the shore,
first one, then another, and many more
breaking and surging until everything is
as before.—Yet everything is different.

Thus we shadows are seized by a strange unrest
when something tells us that people have traveled on,
that some of the possible ones have gotten free.

Ferry Song, 1941

Man, the Great

This poem by Gunnar Ekelöf first appeared in *Ferry Song*, his collection of 1941.

It might appear a strange year to write such a poem, when the triumphant German armies were achieving their greatest victories and when it seemed only a matter of months before they would reach Sweden. But it would be superficial, I feel, to convince oneself that the knowledge of those events is not present in the background of the poem. It is concerned with that *also*.

It was written at a time when Hjalmar Gullberg was allowing the old milestones at Skansen to have their say in poems which, in cautious terms, were meant to tell the Swedish people that they had a national character and freedom to defend,[1] and other poets followed in his tracks. Swedish poetry, which has always had an inclination toward the consolatory, never sought as much consolation as in precisely those years.

It is just that Ekelöf's poem seeks its consolation in a totally unexpected quarter.

It says, quite simply, that we are a small part in a vastly greater, enormously more complex context, which we are unable to comprehend other than as a vague shadow of a notion.

Sigmund Freud's theory of the superego, which steers and links together the blind impulses of the subconscious—which in turn always appears to be in revolt against it—was perhaps a necessary preparation for this poem. The profoundly original aspect about Ekelöf is that he extends the idea by saying that perhaps we ourselves are only one of those blind, half-real impulses in a far greater spiritual life, whose vast scope we shall forever be unable to grasp.

Thus we are kings and rulers over all the blind, incomplete im-

---

1. Hjalmar Gullberg (1898–1961), in his wartime book of poetry, *Fem korn-bröd och två fiskar (Five Loaves of Bread and Two Fishes*, 1942), attempted to boost Swedish morale. Skansen is the park outside Stockholm, whose central purpose has been—through restoration of old buildings and homes, support and exhibition of antiquated crafts and working methods, and staging of folk entertainment—to physically preserve the traditions and spirit of Swedish history.

pulses in ourselves—over all the people we might have become but who, fortunately or unfortunately, we never had the chance to become—and, at the same time, we are no more than such minute impulses in a greater ego.

It must have seemed fairly obvious to combine the second idea with the first at a time when the great, overwhelming experience must have consisted of seeing human beings acting as if transformed, of hearing the language alter its mood and style, down to the most minute detail, in radio news broadcasts. A time when poets, politicians, and ordinary people suddenly seemed to be pulling off their ordinary faces, as if they had been nothing more than a kind of rubber mask, to reveal other, and terrifying, faces. At a time when great masses of people seem to be experiencing inexplicable changes of attitude, it is easier to imagine that they are subjects *themselves*, captives *themselves*

> in some greater being, whose ego and essence
> we comprehend as little as our superior
> his superior. From their death and love
> our own feelings have received a coloring.

There is, in these lines, an echo of the nineteenth century's great historical philosophers, of Hegel and Fichte, thinkers who sought to explain the apparently blind, inexplicable and frightening aspects of world history by maintaining that an equally blind, great consciousness was in the process of finding its own way to clarity through the different cultures, wars, nations, and rebellions.

But there are roots even older than those. The medieval Arabic philosophers were profoundly occupied with the idea of "Man, the Great." In ibn-Sina or, as the Scholastics called him, Avicenna (who died at Hamadan in the year 1037), and in al-Gazali (who died at Nissapour in 1111), there existed a highly developed idea that every individual human consciousness is but an element in a greater, an immense consciousness.

Ekelöf knew these philosophers through his studies in Persian and Arabic religious poetry, and he knew how this heretical idea had influenced a whole mysterious undercurrent in the Arabic poetic tradition.

And hadn't he himself written, in the 1920s, in a singularly raw, melancholy, and, at the same time, self-confident prose fragment which stands as a prelude of sorts to his entire literary career (and which he did not dare to publish until 1965): "I feel the cell, the protozoan within me; after millions upon millions of years, I have found myself again in a human being."

The poem's truly great dimensions perhaps first become apparent in the second stanza, when the only image that has filled the entire first stanza is replaced by another. It is but rarely that a poet invents a genuine, a great, poetic image (and not only a metaphor, that is to say) which is utterly new. But this steamer beyond the horizon, these swells that reach us on the shore, have no direct equivalent in the entire history of poetry.

A fascinating line in the poem is, of course, the third one, where we are likened to kings who reign over the blind mass of impulses and possibilities within us.

On television reports, we occasionally see a shy and slightly awkward young man in a serge suit being chased from one social event to another by reporters and photographers. He is "His Majesty, the King."

In Jungian psychology, as well as in many medieval contexts (in alchemy, for example), "the King" is the symbol for the unity of the ego. Anyone who has seen a modern African king—ceremonious, his iron staff raised as a sign that speaking is permitted, only to be planted down again, resolutely, on the ground, with a ponderous, grave gesture, indicating that all discussion is to cease—would have difficulty escaping the image.

Perhaps it is not only evening newscasters and the editorial departments of weekly magazines that are driving these photographers and reporters. Perhaps they symbolize something within themselves, a loss of the sense of ego, due to their indecorous and inquisitive chasing after that everyday figure in the serge suit who will never be able to supply the answer to the inner enigma that is tormenting them.

Ola Hansson

Skåne IV

Kvava ilar stryka och gå . . .
nu kvällas det hemma i Skåne.
Augustinatten faller på
utan stjärnor och måne.
Man höstar tyst med brådska, —
det drager opp till åska.

På stacken, hög som gårdens tak,
gestaltar tyst sig röra.
Med drängen framtill och pigorna bak
ses sista lasset köra
långt ute på skumma vägar
igenom tomma tegar.

Det skymmer hett, det skymmer blått
på slätt, som andlöst tiger.
Det blixtrar tätt och mullrar smått, —
från havet åskan stiger.
Hem bringas kreaturen . . .
Nu smattrar i eldhav skuren.

Nya visor, 1907

Scania IV

Oppressively, the small gusts come and go . . .
at home in Scania it will be evening soon.
The August night has now begun to show,
devoid of stars, devoid of moon.
In silent haste, the harvester works—
above him the threatening thunderstorm lurks.

As tall as the roof, on top of the stack,
silent shapes are bustling.
The farmhand in front, the maids in the back,
the day's last load is seen rustling
at dusk on roads so far away
through barren fields where once stood hay.

The dusk comes warm, the dusk comes blue
to plain, which breathless, silent, lies.
A lightning swarm, a rumbling brew—
at sea the thunder starts to rise.
Into the barn are led the cattle . . .
In a sea of lightning the hailstones rattle.

New Songs, 1907

Beneath the Threshold of Consciousness

Ola Hansson made the one fatal mistake which can be all too tempting for an author from a struggling minority group in a linguistically and literarily small nation with powerful and rigidly frozen literary institutions: he allowed himself to be carried away by bitterness.

He belongs to the generation of the radical breakthrough, for whom the alternatives consisted of either voluntary exile or obsequiousness before an establishment which, in any event, would never have understood where his true worth lay. Like Strindberg, his misfortune was that the only audience able to appreciate his work—young bourgeois intellectuals with radical ideas—comprised far too thin a stratum, incapable of sustaining a body of literature.

For Strindberg, struggle was, in a way, his natural element. He transformed it into a driving force. For Ola Hansson, the conflict had a much more unfortunate denouement. He died destitute, in exile. The German public, which for a moment appeared to be accepting him, betrayed him after only a few books, when the voguish interest in Scandinavians had dissipated, and the path to bitterness then became all the more conspicuous.

The critic Fredrik Böök, who was one of his many enemies, has said that the bitterness diluted and damaged the wonderful originality and sensualism in Hansson's poetry, and, unfortunately, there is something to this. It's just that Fredrik Böök was altogether the wrong person to say it.

Ola Hansson was weaker than Strindberg. He was unable to extricate himself from the struggle. Like a caged hamster on a wheel, he raced around in injustice and in the contempt he sought to mobilize against his unfair judges.

The Nietzschean hate poems in his later works contain a social indignation which was not cheaply won; he speaks, for example, of large estates where women are still being hitched up to the plow. But there are also poems which show that he has not read his beloved Nietzsche thoroughly enough to perceive how necessary it also is to forget one's enemies.

For half a century now, this development has totally obscured his greatness as a poet.

It is quite a pity.

There is a category of poets—Ekelöf was certainly one of them—who seem to have more direct access to their own subconscious than do other people. In Ola Hansson, this is manifested by a connection between landscape and spiritual life so immediate that it is virtually impossible to separate one from the other and by a nervous sensitivity for that one exact element in the landscape which cannot be expressed in words but which is, nonetheless, the sum total of the entire experience.

"Mood" is a foolish word, because it so strongly associates the entire phenomenon with the most sentimental aspects of German romanticism. But surely we have all experienced that singular *character of wholeness* in a situation.

You leave a room. You set off for a walk. When you return, the room is somehow different.

Ola Hansson knew a great deal about these things. In certain respects one can say that he became a follower of the subconscious as one follows a particular life style.

He did not have much faith in rational deliberation, in the type of reasoning which is normally assumed to comprise the basis for decisions men make, for actions they take. He writes the following:

> Certainly these events pass through the consciousness. But, before they are able to arrive there, they have gone through an entire process of germinating and taking root beneath the threshold of consciousness. This is also the reason why so many resolutions, which are pure products of thought, are not carried through at the last moment, because something completely different and opposite occurs which is as great a surprise for the person concerned as for those around him.

The most striking feature of the poem is the silent, the *dreamlike* silent, character of the hurrying harvesters. The figures moving about on top of the tall stack have something about them which is just as threatening as the thunderstorm which, with its violent sounds, will ultimately break the nervous tension. The wind gusts, signs of approaching thunder, which come and go and—as is always the case with the very first gusts preceding a violent storm—do not seem to want to take hold; the wagons on the narrow, darkening roads, with the farmhand placed up front and the maids in back, in an ancient, almost hierarchical order: everything is described with swift, exquisite precision, and everything is described *as if* it were concerned with something else.

In Ola Hansson, just as in Vilhelm Ekelund, there is a hostility toward the all too regular meter, a need to create irregularities, rhythmical countermovements in the poetic line.

In masterly fashion, Hansson breaks the mainly iambic rhythm in his poem with trochees, which blow up like small, threatening gusts of wind.

To the dreamlike atmosphere of the poem belongs the peculiar distance at which he holds its inhabitants from the eye of the reader. They move about, small as ants, in their landscape; they are not individual people but a collective, like that of the anthill. There is nothing aggressive or deprecatory in this. It seems to be this poem's natural focal distance from reality.

This anonymous collective is made up of the people among whom Ola Hansson grew up. Scanian small farmers. He knows how they speak, he knows how that bustling harvest, before the thunderstorm, feels. They are as familiar to him as water to a fish.

A single word in the poem, "home," in the second line, reveals that the entire scene is a memory. It is a memory picture conjured up by some sultry thundershowers, somewhere outside a hotel room window in a foreign country.

From a vague recollection, hardly more than the memory of a wind, the impression of reality in the poem is increased to a more and more detailed picture and, by the time the poem's violent culmination is reached, the narrator is already deep within the landscape.

This is how the subconscious works. This is how an entire process can germinate and take root beneath the threshold of consciousness.

Göran Printz-Påhlson

När Beaumont och Tocqueville först besökte Sing-Sing

När Beaumont och Tocqueville först besökte Sing-Sing
för att samla material till sin avhandling om fångvården i Amerika,
såg de liksom en vision av framtidens värld.

Fångarna som utan bojor arbetade sida vid sida
i dov tystnad, förenade i ordlöst hat,
vakterna, som på randen av en vulkan,
behärskande sin panik med håglöst våld,
de mörka husen, halvfärdiga cellblock.

Så korrumperades inför deras ögon genom årtionden
    drömmen om Amerika
korvstånd sprang upp som fotspår på leriga vägar,
annonsskyltar trängdes i beundran kring utsikterna,
indianen sålde smilande suvenirer från Woolworths.

Och Natty Bumppo som kommer hem från kontoret
i vag förtvivlan över att inga vidder finns mer att besegra,
kontrollerar att inga grannar brutit sig in för att stjäla,
ser i garderoberna efter ryssar och judar och sätter på TV:n,
sätter sig ner och skisserar ett hatbrev till insändarspalten.

De tysta, okedjade fångarna: det är en dröm
som skall plåga Europa i namnlösa nätter,
värre än skräcken för kaos, och verkligare.

Gradiva, 1966

When Beaumont and Tocqueville First Visited Sing-Sing

When Beaumont and Tocqueville first visited Sing-Sing
to gather material for their treatise on the penal system in America,
they saw a vision of the world of the future.

The prisoners, working without shackles, side by side
in dull silence, united by wordless hatred,
the guards, as if on the rim of a volcano,
controlling their panic through indolent violence,
the dark houses, half-finished cellblocks.

Then, through the decades, before their eyes, was corrupted the
    dream of America
hotdog stands emerged like footprints on muddy roads,
billboards crowded in admiration around the scenic drives,
smiling, the Indian sold souvenirs from Woolworth's.

And Natty Bumppo, coming home from the office
in vague despair because there are no more expanses to conquer,
checks to see that no neighbors have broken in to steal,
looks in the closets for Russians and Jews and turns on the TV,
sits down and drafts a hate letter to the editor.

Those silent, unchained prisoners: it is a dream
which will torment Europe for nameless nights,
worse than the fear of Chaos, and more real.

Gradiva, 1966

The World as Prison

This poem can be found in *Gradiva*, Göran Printz-Påhlson's book of collected poems from 1966. One of the years of the war in Vietnam, when Swedish public opinion had cause to occupy itself intensely with the matter of American democracy and its development.

On May 10, 1831, two young Frenchmen landed in New York. They were Alexis de Tocqueville and Gustave de Beaumont, jurists from the court of law at Versailles who had been charged by the French government with the task of studying the penal system in America. Their journey, which was to last until February 1832, was extraordinarily extensive; they observed institutions, spoke with hundreds of persons, and filled endless travel diaries. Eventually, their trip would give rise to two famous writings in the area of political science: a collaborative book on the American prison system (1832) and Tocqueville's classic work on American democracy, *La Démocratie en Amérique* (1835).

Most vivid are their travel diaries. In September 1831 they visited Sing-Sing, the most famous experimental prison of that time. Tocqueville says the following:

> The prison system, as it is set up at Sing-Sing, seems to me dangerous to apply [in France]. This is the reason: without a doubt, the discipline in Sing-Sing is infinitely better than anything resembling it in France. Its results are:
> 1. The health of the prisoners
> 2. Their extreme concentration at work
> 3. The income the State receives from their work
> 4. *Perhaps* that a certain number of them are improved morally
> How are these results obtained? Through the total *silence*, which isolates the prisoners from one another, and the unceasing *labor*, which absorbs their physical and moral strength. How is a sufficient degree of *silence* and *labor* achieved? Through the power, which has been given to all the guards, to administer corporeal punishment according to their own caprice. . . . The fact that this discipline is maintained is the only tie that binds them. . . . We saw 250 prisoners in a quarry, breaking stones. These men,

placed under special guard, had all committed violent crimes, which indicated that they were of a character one had particular reason to fear. On all sides of each of them lay sledgehammers. Three unarmed guards walked about in the quarry. Their eyes were restless the entire time.

There are poems which consist of metaphors—many, perhaps exquisite metaphors—which slowly but surely lead the reader in whichever direction the poet desires. And there are poems which, in their entirety, consist of one single metaphor. Göran Printz-Påhlson's poem is of the latter variety. What Beaumont and Tocqueville saw in Sing-Sing he transforms into a metaphor for an entire world, a prison without shackles, where only fear, discipline, routine—or whatever we may call it—keep people at their work; and, perhaps most important, this fear is mutual.

In the final analysis, this profoundly political poem is not directed so much against the United States. It is concerned with industrial society as a whole.

The unchained prisoners: in the beginning of the 1830s, penal reforms were instituted in a number of civilized countries. A prison system with medieval roots, as we know of it from, for example, the old Swedish fortresses with their confined and idle prisoners, was replaced by a new system, based less on shackles and more on the idea of hard, disciplined labor. Quite often there was a political-economical motivation alongside the humanizing thought, marked by a deep puritanism, underlying it.

In his sociological study, *Surveiller et punir* (1975), Michel Foucault has shown that even the great liberal, Jeremy Bentham, tends to view the prison as a branch of the industrial system; Bentham dreams of a reformed and modernized prison system, where convicts are gradually transferred to industrial production, which is of benefit to society. A modern observer has noted that one need only see the gate system of a modern large industrial complex to obtain a clear understanding of the similarity.

From a statistical point of view, in the normal Western industrial nations, it is an ever-diminishing, tiny portion of the general population which ends up in prison. Yet this particular human situation fascinates us more than all others. Perhaps, as Foucault has pointed out, because this is the point where power in society becomes most nakedly manifest.

The chainless, silent prisoners in Printz-Påhlson's poem, and their frightened guards with the nervous, worried eyes, are thus meant to function as a metaphor for an industrial society, in which all shackles have been internalized and people are kept in their place through fear of one another.

Natty Bumppo, who comes home from the office and begins to search for Russians and Jews in his closets, the everyday person without hope and without any other course of action than sterile terror of his equally frightened peers, is made to symbolize the condition which is the bitter fruit of industrialism: fascism.

The world transformed into a prison: the poem is part of a sequence entitled *Carceri Suite*. This name alludes to a series of engravings by the eighteenth-century Italian artist, Piranesi, a remarkable suite of gigantic, labyrinthine prisons, an indoor universe of deep arches and endless cavities of hewn stone.

Printz-Påhlson's work has the same melancholy authority, the same desolate, windy dream quality—*dream* and yet, *reality*:

worse than the fear of Chaos, and more real.

Georg Stiernhielm

Oppå Astrild, som står och slipar sine pilar

Slipstenen intet skär; men skärper pilar och yxor:
samma natur min käresta bär; hon skärper och vässer
älskogen i mitt bröst; men själv är hon stumpar' än vätsten.
Mitt stolt' hjärta då gör hon vekt och sårar i älskog;
själver osargat och hel är hårdare flinto.
Själver är hon is och snö; men mig är hon hetar' än elden.
Kall är hon av sig själv; men mig hon bråder i älskog.
Allt vad hon yrker och gör, hon själv vart känner ell' av-vet:
mild är hon och spisar ut det hon själv vart äger ell' åtte.

1640-talet

On Astrild, Honing His Arrows

The grindstone can never cut; but it sharpens arrows and axes:
of similar nature is my beloved; she sharpens and hones
great love in my breast; herself she is duller than whetstone.
My proud heart she then weakens and wounds in its love,
while hers, safe and sane, is harder than flintstone.
She herself is ice and snow; to me she is hotter than fire.
Frigid is she by nature; but me she does hurry to love her.
All she occasions and does, by her is unfelt or unknown:
mild is she and gives away what she neither owns nor ever was hers.

1640s

At the Grindstone of Love

Pondering over older Swedish poetry, one is often struck by how *late* the entire history of this poetry is, how *recently* everything actually occurred. Even a Kellgren (Johan Henrik, 1751–1795) or a Lidner (Bengt, 1757–1793) is almost our contemporary, from a broader literary-historical perspective.

As far as the ballads, Swedish Renaissance poetry, and the Lutheran hymns are concerned, we know, of course, that all of them are greatly dependent upon foreign models; albeit Swedish, they nonetheless belong to another culture. And the same applies, obviously, to the medieval Latin poems.

It is during the Period of Great Power, around the middle of the seventeenth century, that the necessary, decisive steps forward—toward a Swedish poetry—are taken. By this time, Petrarch's sonnets and Cavalcanti's canzones, not to mention the poetry of the Provençal, already form part of a distant European past. Echoes, shadow effects, distorted signals are reaching forth from a period of flowering in European poetry which is already long gone.

In the 1640s, a struggle is being waged, about which little is now ever said, but which is critical and will eventually be decisive for the entire course Swedish poetry will take all the way up to the moment European modernism slowly reaches us, by way of Finland and Germany, far into the twentieth century.

It is the settling of accounts between two great poetic principles, where one will be victorious and the other irrevocably vanquished. Italian Renaissance poetry, like Latin verse, was *syllabic*; that is, the metrical foot was based upon syllable length and the line on syllable number. This principle reached us, through German models most often, and we still find a shadow of it in Skogekär Bergbo's love sonnets in *Wenerid.*

Bergbo, or Gustaf Rosenhane, who was most probably the man behind the sonnets, was a poet in imitation of the Renaissance. In him one can still perceive the possibilities of a different Swedish poetic development, one which was never realized. Had it been, we would be living in a world where Carl Snoilsky's (1841–1903) reel rhythms and Gustaf Fröding's (1860–1911) exquisite, ringing vowels would never have existed but where it would probably have been possible for Strindberg's *Sömngångarnätter* (*Somnambulist Nights*, 1884) to be created.

A poetry based on syllable length is blessed with tremendous technical advantages. It provides softness, sharpness; it allows the intellect to come forth, almost nakedly, in the poem. The marvelous, dry sharpness in a Petrarch or a Cavalcanti, like a surgeon's knife, exists as a possibility in the syllabic poem.

But the writing and rhyming students, clerics, and merchants who, in the Uppsala and Stockholm of the 1640s, sought to fashion a Swedish poem based upon the counting of syllables were not great poets or, in any case, were not great enough to conquer the reluctance of the material.

The second principle is well-known: base the metrical foot on the degree of stress in the syllable, not on its length. It was this principle that emerged victorious.

At the critical moment, it is a poet with all-overshadowing authority who will be decisive. That poet is Stiernhielm. With a point of departure in classical, fixed poetic measure—above all, the hexameter—he creates a Swedish poetry which is the *translation* of the hexameter into a system where stress replaces length.

In a fine book, *Vers och språk i vasatidens och stormaktstidens svenska diktning* (*Verse and Language in the Swedish Poetry of the Wasa Period and the Period of Great Power*, 1975), Professor Carl Ivar Ståhle has shown just *how* great Stiernhielm's influence actually was. Stiernhielm's poem "Hercules" (1658) and its introductory line about the hero, who arises one morning in early youth, "laden with anguish and doubt as to how his life he now should begin," [1] are subsequently echoed in many verses during the decade after its appearance.

Stiernhielm is able to imbue Swedish with a kind of poetic authority. His talent is solid, powerful, lightning fast. He is, in one way, a poet without finesse, but he is also a poet without hesitation. One might wonder what would have become of him if, for example, he had been born in the France of the same time and were not—as it eventually turned out—invested with the thankless mission of clearing a path for others in the rocky and difficult to plow fields of seventeenth-century Swedish.

1. "Fuller av ångest och twijk huru han skulle sitt leverne börja."

He accomplishes his great task in an authoritarian, almost brutal fashion. But he accomplishes it. There is a singing quality about everything he has done—it is living poetry; the solid dialect of his native Dalecarlia can be heard right through the lines.

There is somewhat of a tradition, or a main furrow, of *complaining* in Swedish poetry. An enormous amount of it deals with the idea that man is small and weak, that he is not able to muster very much against stronger forces, that life is painful, and that everything is in vain. Stiernhielm finds himself outside this tradition. There is never any complaining in his poetry and if, on the surface, it seems a complaint, it is quickly transformed into something else.

"On Astrild" is a bagatelle, a little ballet poem. Linguistically, it is so far removed from modern Swedish that some important words must be explained before we can enjoy it fully.

"Stumpar" (here translated as "duller") should, of course, be "stummare." Stiernhielm allows the final syllable to drop off so that the number of syllables will fit the pattern of the classical hexameter; such expeditious cuts are often made by his contemporaries, and the lesser poets do so with considerably greater ruthlessness than he. In comparison with the classical meter, which is now gaining a foothold, the leisurely seventeenth-century Swedish language frequently looks like a Procrustean bed. "Hårdare flinto" means "hårdare *än* flinta" ("harder than flintstone"): here there linger traces of a time when the Swedish noun had just as many cases as the German. "Bråder," in the half line "men mig hon bråder i älskog" ("but me she does hurry to love her"), is difficult to translate into modern Swedish. Perhaps one should say "hon bryr mig" ("she worries me")? But, in so doing, one loses the ardor, the urgency—in short, that which constitutes the passion itself.

The final two lines will be completely incomprehensible if one does not understand that the word "vart" means "varken" ("neither") and that the last word in the poem, "åtte," must be translated into today's Swedish as "ägde" ("owned"—translated here as "was hers"). These are not great difficulties. As a rule, a reader fluent in modern Swedish doesn't even require a dictionary; rather, a moment or two of reflection will usually be sufficient. From a linguistic perspective, Stiernhielm is perhaps one step more difficult than Skogekär Bergbo, who writes in such a gentlemanly fashion and with such refinement that it is almost impossible to identify his place in history from his language. In no case should the minor linguistic problems prevent anyone from deriving pleasure from the poetry of Sweden's Period of Great Power, with its resonance, its freshness, its drastic humor.

How infrequently we come across a poet who speaks of this not all too rare love situation with such inimitable self-irony!

"On Astrild" exemplifies an interesting poetic technique. It is dominated by a single, central metaphor: the grindstone which sharpens other objects and, itself, remains silent and dull. This metaphor subsequently divides itself into many smaller ones: ice and fire, generosity and miserliness. Everything is based upon the original contrasting pair.

A portrait develops, not of a woman but of a kind of erotic relationship, which it seems one has seen many times before.

And this all takes on a terribly droll quality, because one gets a powerful impression that, if the desired one were permitted to speak, she would most assuredly offer a completely disparate version.

It is a stroke of genius, of course, to compare erotic passion to the keenness of an edged tool. The number of original poetic metaphors in this world is small, considerably smaller than it may seem, for so many of them in the European poetic tradition, far into modernism, consist essentially of the conversions of a finite stock of metaphors— through translations and transformations—into constantly new contexts.

In Georg Stiernhielm, such metaphors as these frequently stem from one or another German or Dutch emblem book. But he *makes* them new. He is working with a language which has not yet been crisscrossed by other poetic travelers. He is journeying through virgin territory and seeing everything with fresh eyes.

Vilhelm Ekelund

Det första vårregnet

Som ett nät av svarta spindelvävar
hänga trädens våta grenar.
I den tysta februarinatten
sjunger sakta, klingar, svävar
fram ur däldens snår och stenar
suset av en källas vatten.

I den tysta februarinatten
gråter himlen stilla.

Syner, 1901

The First Spring Rain

Black, like webs from spinning spiders playing
branches, moisture-heavy, bend
In the silent February night
singing slowly, ringing, swaying
out of rock-strewn, brushy glen
sounds of wellspring, watery delight.

In the silent February night
cry the heavens softly.

Visions, 1901

The Reality between the Words

For the average Swede, Ekelund's poetry can occasionally take on an exotic quality, which comes about quite simply because his Scanian landscape truly *is* a foreign landscape. Our everyday experiences mean more to our relationship with a poem than we would normally imagine.

I remember how, while teaching Tomas Tranströmer to students at the University of Texas, I came to the well-known line that reads: "like a sun-warm stone in my hand" ("som en solvarm sten i handen").

"That can't be," one of the students said immediately. "If somebody were to hold a 'sun-warm stone' in his hand, he'd get blisters. And he'd toss that stone away as fast as he possibly could."

Undoubtedly, this is how stones and men behave in the parched regions around Texas' Colorado River. Of course, that did not prevent the student from understanding what Tranströmer meant. I think the poem even became more interesting to him when he understood that this brief picture contained a wholly alien climatic experience.

For a reader from central or northern Sweden, February is a period of deep snow and dryness; arctic-clear days, when bullfinches and silktails come out from the deep woods in search of food; ice-cold nights, when contraction brought on by the chill causes a moaning and groaning in wooden houses, and shoes crunch on unplowed roads.

For Ekelund, "the silent February night" is the time when the landscape begins to shed silent tears. I think that a northern Swedish reader would more readily associate this experience with the beginning of April.

Differences which do not mean anything and, yet, most profoundly *do* mean something. They compel us to make an extra effort, and in this small exertion there is always a gain, a small electrical charge. I know of no more sterile an idea than that poetry should sneak up as close to its reader as possible, make itself as accessible as possible to him. The little difference in electric potential itself—the one that makes it possible for the spark to leap between anode and cathode— will, of course, be lost in that way.

Ekelund's February night, then, is not our February night. It belongs to central Europe; spring nights in Berlin parks are like this: he must have seen such branches, felt that kind of wetness, countless times during his lengthy exile.

I do not think there is any Swedish poet who manifests such firmly rooted opposition, antipathy, obstinate refusal, heightened loathing toward lightly flowing, melodic poetry as does Vilhelm Ekelund. All his contempt for the stale Establishment poetry which dominated the Swedish scene in his youth is present, concealed, in his rhythms.

Nowadays, when free verse is frequently but an expression of the fact that the poet has never learned, or even become acquainted with, any other poetic technique, such verse, in the happiest cases, is created by coincidence.

Among now-living Swedish poets there are precious few who actually take pains to write free verse which is, at the same time, *rhythmically interesting*. In Göran Sonnevi one can recognize such an endeavor, but he is an exception. On the whole, one must go to the great Finland-Swedish poets, to a Diktonius or a Björling, to find anything similar to this.

"The First Spring Rain" begins quite monotonously with two long series of trochees, almost like a ticking clock; even better, like drops— yes, of course, drops falling from branches:

dá-dit-dá-dit-dá-dit-dá-dit-dá-dit
dá-dit-dá-dit-dá-dit-dá-dit

Note that there is one trochee less in the second line. Ekelund is poet enough to know what Petrarch and Dante also knew; *regularity* does not necessarily preclude *irregularity*. It is precisely in the monotony that one can prepare the real surprises. From this uniform, discreetly rhymed trochaic verse the words *February night* free themselves like great beings, slowly and silently advancing creatures.

What occurs in the next line is very typical of Ekelund's entire poetic technique:

singing slowly, ringing, swaying

One *adjective* is seldom enough, and here one *verb* is not enough.

Ekelund takes his time, he specifies exactly, through a series of words, the sensation he wishes to encircle. Because of this, it would be easy, even if we did not know when or by whom it was written, to see that this is a poem written on the threshold of Swedish poetic modernism.

From a classical point of view—that is to say, proceeding from the poetics which have their roots in the French classics—in Boileau's poetic theory there is always one word which is the correct one, and the trick consists in finding that word. Poetry becomes a kind of sharpshooting at reality, with the help of words.

In order for such a poetic technique to appear practicable and reasonable and effective, one must be convinced, naturally, that language really coincides with reality, and it is precisely upon this condition that French classicism builds.

The dissolution, the dejection, begins with romanticism and reaches its culmination during the second half of the nineteenth century, when a succession of philosophers—such as Nietzsche, Fritz Mauthner, and Alexander Bryan Johnson—state plainly that language is not simply approximative: it has nothing at all to do with reality.

This linguistic pessimism penetrates deep into literature during the second half of the nineteenth century. We can already see it in Henrik Ibsen's *The Wild Duck* (1884), with its conviction that human beings cannot possibly live without their illusions, without the "life lie."

And it forms one of the deepest roots for what is usually termed literary modernism. What language can best do with reality is not to reproduce it but, rather, to encircle it through circuitous operations.

This is exactly what is occurring when Ekelund writes:

singing slowly, ringing, swaying

The line produces an enormously effective intensification, but it also evokes an uncertainty, and nature becomes spiritual. It is impossible to differentiate between the state of one's soul and the landscape in "The First Spring Rain," and this is the second characteristic of the poem that obviously connects it with poetic modernism. It is even possible that at bottom it is *exactly the same thing* as saying that the essential element seems to lie between the words rather than in them, but to explain why would take us too far.

The poem is a story about a landscape, but it is at once and in the same context a story about a human being who, after disappointments, impoverishment, and bitterness, suddenly discovers that there are new, life-giving forces in the very midst of the impoverishment and the nakedness. There is a wellspring in the leafless February forest. The rain is not merely rain, it is a crying, exactly as the rain cries in the great French symbolists and, above all, in Paul Verlaine. In all stillness, a change is being readied, the soul is awakening from a period of bitterness, and this must of necessity change the landscape in its entirety. Image and eye coincide. We are what we see, and thus we are changed.

"The First Spring Rain" fits into a great European tradition which, having become a reality, will not permit itself to be forgotten.

Gunnar Björling

Snön och som på en skogsstig
vit
i rymd ett sus
och här
och för en timme sedan
och tassande en liten ljusbrun hund
och som stjärnor blänker täckta lyktors ljus
snart ökar blott i rymden stormvinds brus
snön och som på en skogsstig
vit.

Angelägenhet, 1940

The snow and as if on a forest path
white
in space a soughing
and here
and an hour ago
and padding by a small light-brown dog
and like stars the lights of covered lanterns glow
soon only in space the storm wind's roar will grow
the snow and as if on a forest path
white.

Concern, 1940

Play with the Unuttered

The most striking feature in Gunnar Björling's poem, of course, is that it does not follow conventional grammar. There is only one gramatically complete sentence in the entire poem, the third line from the end, and it enters the poem in such a manner that it sounds like a reminiscence of something else—not really a quote but a rhetorical echo of poetry in general, an echo that quickly dies away once again.

The poem's first line contains a noun, "snow," which actually stands there, large and quiet, like the snow itself. And then the line continues with what appears to be the beginning of a poetic metaphor, introduced by "as if," the perpetual adhesive words between the poetic image and the thing imagined.

Except that the image is not completed. We never get to know the second element in the image. Exactly what was to be compared with this forest path is not made explicit.

In almost all contexts where language appears as writing, we meet a grammatically complete language. But in the conversations people have on trains and buses, in the marital bed, and, above all, in the conversations we constantly conduct with ourselves, linguistically well formed sentences are actually just as rare as in this poem.

It is solely from the perspective of the written language that syntax dominates our thinking. The overwhelming majority of the sentences we formulate during the course of a lifetime are just as fragmentary, as incomplete, and are characterized by the same lack of respect for parts of speech as Björling's poetic landscape.

We think half in images, half in words, and how often doesn't a thought come to a halt in the middle of an image, in precisely the same fashion as in Björling's first line. Occasionally, perhaps, because the thought did not *want* to lead any further, but just as often because no more was *required* of it. In the vague and quiet conversations we secretly carry on with ourselves in ordinary situations, that which goes unuttered is often just as real and just as expressive as that which is uttered.

Gunnar Björling's poetry, perhaps the most classically modernistic in the Swedish language, is thus quite realistic in that it gives the *unuttered* approximately the same dominant position it occupies in ordinary spoken language. It is when we compare it with standard written language that it looks peculiar.

Now it would certainly be a mistake to think that Björling is striving for some kind of colloquial quality in his poem. Its language is, in actuality, refined and artistic, just as thoroughly considered, just as beautiful in form, as a classical sonnet. What unites the poem with those words we usually mumble to ourselves in grammatically disorganized fragments is only that the unuttered plays just as great a role as the uttered in the poem.

Among many other things, the poem proves (as does most of what Björling has written) that free verse can be at least equally as rigorous as fixed-form poetry. One could even say that Björling's poems, for the most part, contain a fixed form, not one that is repeated but, rather, one that remains unique to each poem.

There exists a special kind of intimacy in a winter day. In the midst of the chill and the whiteness, one is able to repose quietly, in a different way than one ever can in the summer sun, accompanied by the soughing of swaying treetops.

It is the intimate quiet, the tranquility of the new snow, that Björling elicits. Note the line:

and like stars the lights of covered lanterns glow

It is never said, but it is nevertheless obvious, of course, that the lanterns are covered because snow has fallen over them. The warm and cozy stillness of new-fallen snow enshrouds the entire poem. And the new snow is so clean that it is as undisturbed as snow on a forest path. In this snow, the furtive passing of a small brown dog becomes an occurrence worth noting, but this padding-by also becomes an important element of the stillness.

The remarkable drawing together of a spatial concept, which occurs in the line consisting of the words "and here," and a temporal concept in the next line, "and an hour ago," is extremely suggestive. It creates the impression of a kind of ubiquitousness. Both here and somewhere else. Both now and then. Throughout the entire history of poetic modernism, this feature constantly recurs: a need to bring places together into one single place, moments into one single moment. A kind of need to create, with the help of art, experiences of totality which do not exist in the natural world.

The poem begins calmly, almost statically. The few words fall in drops, one after the other. A picture of a snowy landscape is precipitated, in which then and now and, simultaneously, great and small (compare the dog's role in the poem with the role the word "space" plays there) are united.

But after the sixth line—where the little padding dog appears—something happens.

There come two long trochaic lines, rhetorically singing and reverberant, which deal with the starlight from the lanterns and the brewing storm. The poem suddenly grows large, animated; it acquires a tone not unlike a suite for cello by Bach. One suspects that the initial lines contained tremendous restrained energies. What kind of emotion do these long melodic lines actually express? Is it positive or negative? Is it a matter of some kind of despair, a sudden realization of the futility of everything? Or is it, on the contrary, happiness over the impending storm, a feeling of communion with a great cosmic context?

Personally, I must confess that I am unable to reach any uniform conclusion. The entire poem is concerned with intense emotions, but these emotions are never mentioned by name, no labels are pinned on them. Because of this, Björling's poem is just as realistic as is the matter of incomplete syntax. After all, how often, in reality, are we able to say, offhand, whether we are experiencing happiness or sorrow?

That kind of cocksureness is reserved almost exclusively for characters in novels.

At the end of the poem, its first two lines return, identical in every respect. This provides an impression of great compactness. We have witnessed an inner event, one of those delicate, difficult to define movements of the soul, which words ordinarily merely graze lightly, a small slide, a slight change in the subconscious.

And now everything is just as still as before.

Erik Johan Stagnelius

Till förruttnelsen

Förruttnelse, hasta, o älskade brud,
  att bädda vårt ensliga läger!
Förskjuten av världen, förskjuten av Gud
  blott dig till förhoppning jag äger.
Fort, smycka vår kammar—på svartklädda båren
  den suckande älskarn din boning skall nå.
Fort, tillred vår brudsäng—med nejlikor våren
  skall henne beså.

Slut ömt i ditt sköte min smäktande kropp!
  Förkväv i ditt famntag min smärta!
I maskar lös tanken och känslorna opp,
  i aska mitt brinnande hjärta!
Rik är du, o flicka!—i hemgift du giver
den stora, den grönskande jorden åt mig.
Jag plågas häruppe, men lycklig jag bliver
  därnere hos dig.

Till vällustens ljuva, förtrollande kvalm
  oss svartklädda brudsvenner följa.
Vår bröllopssång ringes av klockornas malm
  och gröna gardiner oss dölja.
När stormarna ute på världshavet råda
när fasor den blodade jorden bebo,
när fejderna rasa, vi slumra dock båda
  i gyllene ro.

senast 1818

To Putrefaction

Putrefaction, hasten, Oh beloved bride,
   to ready our lonely lover's couch!
By the world rejected, by God set aside
   thou art my only hope, I vouch.
Quick! our chamber now adorn—on bier of somber decorations
   the sighing lover to your dwelling shall go.
Quick! prepare the bridal bed—soon springtime's gift of new
  carnations
   shall over her grow.

Caress in thy womb my body, which yearns!
   In thine embraces smother my pain!
My thoughts and my feelings dissolve into worms,
   of my burning heart let but ashes remain!
Rich art thou, o maid!—in dowry dost give
  the vast, the verdurous earth to me.
Up here do I suffer, but happy shall live
   down there with thee.

To stifling, enchanting realms of desire
   black-velvet pages lead bridegroom and bride.
Our nuptial hymn chiming bells will attire
   and curtains of green will both of us hide.
When out on the oceans tempests prevail,
when terrors will not bloodied earth release,
when battles are raging, in slumber we'll sail
   in aureate peace.

no later than 1818

The Wisdom of Stagnelius

It is somewhat remarkable to see how hurriedly, how discreetly and cautiously, the different Stagnelius biographers rush past his poem, "To Putrefaction."

In the first of Fredrik Böök's three Stagnelius studies, the monumental, over five hundred pages long *Erik Johan Stagnelius* (1919), the poem figures in only two places. In the first place, it receives no elaboration whatsoever, and in the second, it is described as "the hymn which Stagnelius, in a moment of guilt and forlornness, addressed 'To Putrefaction.'"

Böök is in no way unique in this reaction. One of the very first readers, the poet's father, Bishop Magnus Stagnelius of Kalmar, who was normally extremely reverent with regard to his son's manuscripts —which were entrusted to him—felt compelled to insert a revision in the third line of the first stanza. Thus, in his edition, it is not "by God set aside" ("förskjuten av Gud") but, instead, "but not by God" ("men inte av Gud").

In other words, different, more or less kindred readers have been embarrassed by this poem in Stagnelius' behalf. It has been declared brilliant but sick, very sick. References have been made to Stagnelius' unfortunate fate as a poet, his constant physical pain, his abuse of alcohol and opium, his erotic isolation.

Since no one has ever been able to deny its enormous beauty, the brilliance in its fusing together of two metaphorical worlds—the entire literary machinery of death of the baroque, and that of the connubial bed—with all the paraphernalia of worms, black-clad wedding pages, and carnations (carnations were used to anesthetize worshippers to the stench of putrefaction emanating from the crypts inside the church), the poem has remained a literary scandal.

The reasons for this are, naturally, manifold. One is the gross transgression of the rules of religious remorse, inherent in the words "by God set aside." Another is the rare explicitness, even for the romantic period, of the sexual images.

Caress in thy womb my body, which yearns!

Exactly what sort of embrace Stagnelius had in mind couldn't have puzzled a contemporary reader.

But the situation during Stagnelius' time is not the same as at the time of Fröding's "En morgondröm" ("A Morning Dream," 1896).[1] The poem's essential offensiveness lies in the bringing together of sexual intercourse with putrefaction and death.

It is this juxtaposition that constrains critics, far into the twentieth century, to forgive the poem by maintaining that it was written in despair.

They hardly notice the inconsistency that arises as a result of this. Despair is a complicated emotion which, in different human and historical contexts, can mean almost anything. With the knowledge we possess about Stagnelius' private existence (and it was, particularly toward the end of his life, so degenerate that even tolerant observers preferred to maintain a certain distance), we can calmly draw the conclusion that despair must have occurred in his life, exactly as you and I and just about any housewife in Des Moines experience despair from time to time.

But "Erik Johan Stagnelius" is not merely a slowly deteriorating civil servant in one of the Swedish governmental departments of the early nineteenth century. "Erik Johan Stagnelius" is also the mightiest, the most singular, the most widely ramified text corpus in Swedish romanticism. A thousand delicate, subterranean root fibers connect this literary body to our own language, to our own thoughts. Words are effective. A master of Stagnelius' dimensions does not act coquettishly. If we attempt to brush aside his hymn to putrefaction by pointing to the private existence and private despair of the civil servant in the Ministry of Education and Ecclesiastical Affairs, Erik Johan Stagnelius, the reason is most likely that the poem knows something about us, something, that is, we do not know and, what's more,

---

1. This poem by Gustaf Fröding (1860–1911), which appeared in the collection *Stänk och flikar* (*Splashes and Rags*, 1896), led to his trial on charges of immorality because of its frank treatment of the sexual act at a time when Victorian moral attitudes permeated Swedish society. Although he was acquitted, the trial left Fröding a broken man and precipitated the mental illness which characterized his final years.

something we want to push aside, for we suspect that this knowledge, in one way or another, would do something to us.

To reduce Stagnelius' hymn to "despair" is tantamount to denying his entire literary corpus, for there is no place in it for despair. If there is any emotion the *poetic work* "Stagnelius" has no room for, it is despair. Stagnelius remains the great, the supreme consoler among Swedish poets:

> O Man! Wouldst thou learn life's wisdom,
> o, hear me then! The laws are two that rule
> this life. Power to desire
> is the first. Constraint to renounce
> the second. Ennoble unto liberty
> this constraint, and sanctified and reconciled,
> over the orbiting planets of matter,
> shalt thou enter through the gates of honor.[2]

Thus he writes in "Suckarnes Mystèr" ("The Mystery of Sighs," 1821). There is no reason not to believe that the poet meant what he said. And, as long as we cannot prove the opposite, we should ask ourselves seriously: was he right? Did he possess an insight?

This is a sounder, a more normal way to approach the poem than asking whether the insight was "gnostically inspired." If the professor behind the lectern makes paramount the question of the element of Gnostic philosophy in Stagnelius' poetry, he can easily create the impression that the problem posed by the poem does not concern us.

Between this attitude and the one that advises us to swallow a blue pill when beset by existential anguish, there exists a profound affinity.

But anguish is the point at which the possibilities of freedom become manifest, says the sagacious Søren Kierkegaard.

2. Mänska! Vill du livets vishet lära,
   o, så hör mig! Tvenne lagar styra
   detta liv. Förmågan att begära
   är den första. Tvånget att försaka
   är den andra. Adla du till frihet
   detta tvång, och helgad och försonad
   över stoftets kretsande planeter
   skall du ingå genom ärans portar.

We must approach the hymn to putrefaction, then, from this non-professorial point of departure.

What is it that this poem knows about us, that we do not wish to know?

Death, of course. Death—nothing more complicated.

In science fiction, we occasionally come across stories dealing with the way a biochemically advanced culture has rid itself of death by giving the body tissues interminable endurance. Humans live eternally then, and their problems are, first and foremost, a geometrically increasing overpopulation and, second, the weariness with a condition in which gradually every single experience and every single desire will be repeated.

Modern cell physiology teaches us how unrealistic this entire notion actually is. It is not the case that built into the cell nucleus can be found only the complicated cybernetic balance mechanisms that account for the perpetuation of the species. Death is there, too, passed on by heredity. At a certain point, the cell itself releases the substances that lead to its own dissolution.

The message which has been programmed into the genetic information of the cell nucleus is for the race's perpetuation, not for ours. Death is a biological prerequisite for the continued existence of the race.

Putrefaction, that gradual path which leads from living, highly complex molecules of albuminous substances, over the fatty acids' descending slope of unstable connective elements, down to the once again solid world of the inorganic substances, is part of our biochemical being.

> Putrefaction, hasten, Oh beloved bride

"Eroticism," says Georges Bataille, a modern philosopher, "is saying yes to life all the way into death."

Two elements—let us say two sex cells—which fuse into a new entity lose their individual existences in the process. This can be described, naturally, as the death of these elements.

This image, as a metaphor for the brief coalescence of two personalities in sexual intercourse, is perhaps novel, but in that case it still only reinforces an older perception of the orgasm as an act of death, as a temporary cessation of the personal identity.

The poetry of Carl Michael Bellman (1740–1795) is completely permeated by this erotic death symbolism. ". . . a virgin, must I, within these billows die" (". . . skall jag mö, i dessa böljor dö"), as he allows Ulla to say in "Fredman's Epistle 33," describing the journey over to Djurgården. This ambiguity, well known by every connoisseur of Bellman and by every expert in baroque poetry in general, is a key to Stagnelius' hymn but does not explain it.

In the usual baroque playing with death and orgasm, the orgasm is primary, death secondary.

The brilliant—and frightful, if you will—aspect of Stagnelius' hymn is that it *turns the entire metaphor upside down.*

Fearlessly, indeed with fascination, the poet first considers death in its most immediate, most palpable biochemical form as putrefaction.

Then he allows this phenomenon to represent the orgasm.

In so doing, a tremendous turnabout in perspective occurs, unique in the entire history of Swedish poetry.

All too often, Stagnelius is represented as a kind of life's eternal pubescent. The specter of his Amanda poetry is present. The pencil drawing usually reproduced—the youthful portrait by Lars Gustaf Malmberg, kept at the Royal Library—lingers on. It shows a shy, introverted boy, engrossed in a book with his back facing the world.

The late Oscarians (so named for the latter period of the reign of Oscar II, 1872–1907), who debated against the Amanda poetry, forgot that the time of the Napoleonic wars was not the Victorian age.

Stagnelius is no Henry James, who, according to his biographers, never went near a woman; nor is he a Gustaf Fröding, who gazed dreamily into his own pupils—to express it in somewhat Oscarian terms.

In the early biographers, such as J. M. Wimmerstedt, another image emerges, right through the constant presence of the censorship of C. D. af Wirsén, the leading Oscarian "moral guardian": "[Stagnelius'] Psyche did not always soar on fragile, innocent wings, in lofty Uranian spheres; it was, unfortunately, not always a stranger to the unhealthy, devious regions of baser eroticism."

In his third Stagnelius study, *Stagnelius. Liv och dikt* (*Stagnelius: Life and Poetry*, 1954), Böök leads us to believe—on reasonable evidence—that the degenerate high school teacher Zirkelström, in *Pehrs-mässefärden eller Daniels resehändelser* (*The Journey at Saint Peter's Mass, or Daniel's Travel Experiences*), the novel by Samuel Fryxell which appeared in 1824 to 1825, is actually Stagnelius. Opium abuse and sexual debauchery characterize this figure.

Our age has less interest, perhaps, in the private lives of poets. Let us be content with confirming that Stagnelius, in all probability, was a man who knew what an erotic orgy was, even if his knowledge was most likely gained in bordellos.

In so doing, we have arrived at the point whose attainment required that we traverse this all too private sphere. "To Putrefaction" is not a suicidal poem. It is not a Hamlet monologue. It is not at all a reflection by someone who, confronted with life's pain, imagines he prefers death.

The poem does not deal with death as an alternative to something else.

It deals with death itself, death according to the absolute biochemical definition. This death is putrefaction, fatty acids, the rapidly accelerating breakdown of complex molecules into ammonia and nitrogen.

Concerning this, our biochemical demise, Stagnelius says it is part of our life. That this death should become an orgasm is perfectly natural. Just as it is possible to say yes to life all the way into death, it is also possible to say yes to death all the way into life. If we look it boldly enough in the eye, the enigma assumes a circular shape; the answer becomes the question and the question becomes the answer, and they bite one another forever, like the alchemist's snake, in the rear end.

It is at this juncture that a turning point in the poem appears, a turning point which the unprepared reader interprets as *irony*. And rightfully so, for it is irony, not, as may seem at first, a *bitter* irony but, rather, a *cosmic* one.

How closely related this is to the Zen master's sudden, lightning-like insight; the punch that suddenly causes the novice to perceive that *reality is simple*; the archer who, completely without design, suddenly shoots a bull's-eye; Arthur Ashe, when he returns Connors' unstoppable serve from the depths of a moment of absentmindedness!

"The solution to the problem of life manifests itself in the disappearance of the problem," says Ludwig Wittgenstein in his *Tractatus Logico-Philosophicus* (1922).

There occurs a great dialectic breakthrough in the middle of Stagnelius' poem: an emotion is allowed to grow, without fear and without inhibition, until it is actually transformed into its opposite.

The lines that epitomize this breakthrough have nothing mysterious, nothing obscure about them. They are a simple declaration of a simple and completely verifiable fact. Those critics who have shrunk away from the poem and have chosen to regard it as an expression of despair or guilt have, naturally, had difficulty seeing that *these lines are, in fact, meant completely seriously.*

Stagnelius is the greatest mystic in the history of Swedish poetry.

Consequently, it would appear reasonable—when one comes across a poem which is seemingly in conflict with the mystical (and Gnostic) main tendency in his work—to ask oneself what the poem knows, instead of immediately assuming something along the lines of a weak moment in an otherwise rather courageous character.

This requires, however, that one not always proceed from the assumption that the knowledge and the perspective of the poet in question are necessarily more limited than one's own. Swedish literary scholarship often carries an unfortunate legacy from the evolutionary optimism of the late nineteenth century: its feeling of superiority toward that which preceded it. In our best modern scholars, we can observe a resolute struggle against this suggestion. In Böök, this entire self-evident feeling of possessing better judgment lingers on.

Well, all right! Let us assume this is so, for the moment at least. But in which of these lines, then, is something said which is so self-evident and so contradictory that from the entire thought of putrefaction it is able to produce a new, a completely different thought?

> Rich art thou, o maid!—in dowry dost give
> the vast, the verdurous earth to me.

Sandro Key-Åberg

Jag ser ett djur i varje människa
och det är djuret jag är rädd om.

Ja, inte bara ett men många,
var människa är ett djur som vimlar.

Jag känner i din mage kreaturens
suckan och grisarnas klagan.

Det kryper, lirkar under skinnet
av alla pyttesmå i sina sköldar.

En lärka sjunger i ditt öga,
en vessla spanar på din tunga.

Men det är lika fullt av djurskap i
den övre världen under tankens blånad.

Jag ser en räv som slinker genom tankegräset
där piggson fångar adjektiv i flykten,

och ett tankfullt koskap med gröna ögon
som betar i den friska känslogrönskan.

När människan bottnar i sig själv
går hon med tassar genom ängen

och flyter genom sina djupa sjöar
där gälar skänker henne syre.

När människan bottnar i varandra
är det i det djuriska hon bottnar.

Det är ett sorl av böl och pip
som alla är varandras röster.

Så varmt det blåser ifrån alla djuren!
I denna vind bor människan hos varandra.

I see an animal in every man
and it's the animal that I care for.

Yes, not just one, but many,
every man is an animal that teems.

I feel within your stomach the sighs
of cattle and complaints of pigs.

Beneath my skin, a creeping and wriggling
of all the tiny ones in their shields.

Inside your eye a lark is singing,
upon your tongue a weasel searching.

But there is just as much animalship in
the upper world under the bluish intellect.

I see a fox slinking through the grass of thoughts
where the female porcupine catches adjectives in flight,

and a pensive cowship with eyes of green
grazing in the fresh verdure of emotions.

When man reaches bottom in himself
he pads silently through the meadow

and floats through his deep lakes
where gills provide him with oxygen.

When humans touch bottom in each other
it is the animal they are touching.

There is a purl of lowing and chirping
which are all each others' voices.

So warm the wind that blows from all the creatures!
Together, in this wind, lives all of mankind.

Det är det djuriska som för oss samman.
Det är det mänskliga som skiljer oss.

På sin höjd, 1972

It is the animal that brings us together.
it is the human that separates us.

At the Very Most, 1972

93 : *Sandro Key-Åberg*

A Myth Is Turned Inside Out

Friedrich Engels—who not infrequently stands out as a much more original thinker in his correspondence than in his published works—says, in a letter to Karl Marx on December 8, 1882: "That which is originally sacred is what we have taken over from the Animal Kingdom—*the bestial.*" "Beast"—animal. "Bestial"—animalistic. A word in modern Swedish which we find almost exclusively in journalistic reports of violent and shocking crimes: "With animalistic passion." "Die blonde Bestie," Nietzsche says. He most likely had in mind the woman with whom he was involved in a complicated and unhappy relationship, namely the blonde, and basically quite decent, Lou Salomé. But the expression came to symbolize something entirely different after it was stolen by the Nazis.

What all these words and word usages prove is something already well known: there exists in Western culture an intense hatred of animals. The drains in Gothic cathedrals, where gruesomely distorted animal heads belch forth water; the inciting of bears at the court of Charles XII of Sweden; the lions who were persecuted with red-hot tongs. The rooster in our own ABC books is a relic of the living fighting cock customarily awarded to diligent students in medieval French schools.

A trail of persecuted, killed, maimed, psychically torn and battered animals follows our entire civilization, and this trail disappears into the laboratories of our modern hospital industry. There are signs that suggest that our concept horizon is beginning to reach the point where we will be capable of formulating moral concepts even for this. The modern ecological movement might, if it is successful, slowly lead us to such a viewpoint.

But this hatred of animals, of course, also proves something about our equivocal, indeed our hateful, relationship to ourselves. The thrust of propaganda through the millennia has been to tell us that man has two sides, one which is animalistic and one which is not. And to teach us to side with the nonanimalistic against the animalistic.

"Human" connotes "friendly," "intelligent," "rational," "disciplined." "Animalistic" implies "cruel," "dark," "irrational," "unbridled." But what does "animalistic" really *mean*? And what does "human" actually mean? As in so many cases, the words have been explained with each other's help so many times that their implications have become a truth which is accepted without benefit of analysis.

The greatness of Sandro Key-Åberg's philosophical poem consists in his refusal to accept these premises. He turns them all upside down.

> I see an animal in every man
> and it's the animal that I care for.

The animalistic element is at our very depths, and it is when we touch bottom that we realize our good, our friendliest, our most valuable qualities. The creature warmth that unites us with the animals is the most valuable thing we possess.

In the beginning of the 1960s, Arthur Koestler developed a theory concerning the human cerebrum, which separates us from the animals. It was a complicated theory—what science thought of it was never made quite clear—but, on the whole, it sought to explain an ancient mystery.

How can the same being who would refuse to the bitter end to plunge a broad-bladed knife into his neighbor's stomach calmly, methodically, and with great professionalism drop enormous explosive charges, from an altitude of fifty thousand feet, onto the densely inhabited residential quarters of sleeping cities?

Koestler's theory proceeds from the premise that there live two beings, literally, in every breast or, to put it more correctly, in every brain. The one is represented by those brain cells we have in common with the higher mammals—warmly emotional, impulsive centers designed for battle, play, mating, but also equipped with the safety barriers which insure that the playing dog will not attack when its opponent makes a territory-relinquishing gesture or offers up its throat as a sign of submission.

From this warm, friendly, and limited mammal brain there issues neither evil nor technological progress. It is the forebrain, the cerebrum, this strange novelty of biological evolution, that is responsible for all that is profoundly dangerous in man. It possesses an icy chill. It is capable of storing impulses, of delaying them until just the right moment has arrived. It is capable of abstracting, or straining the emotions from our thoughts, so that a solitary, frigid thought remains where, only moments before, there was a hornet's nest of impulses, all pulling in different directions.

It is this being that is capable of opening bomb bay doors over defenseless cities. A faulty construction on the part of nature? A monster? Or a bold biological leap, an adventurous bound that had to be taken?

Sandro Key-Åberg's poem possesses a treacherous simplicity. He speaks as relaxedly as someone you might happen to meet on a bus, and for this reason it takes quite some time before we discover how truly refined the construction of his poem is.

By speaking about something, by stressing it, one produces in almost all linguistic contexts a kind of negative mirror effect. That which is not mentioned, not emphasized, acquires presence precisely on the strength of its absence.

Sandro Key-Åberg exploits this effect in uncommonly dexterous fashion.

The icy chill of sober calculation, the true extent of human loneliness, the steely eyes of technological mass murderers—nothing of this is mentioned in the poem, yet it can all be found there by virtue of its very negation.

Corresponding to this great turnabout is a large number of smaller ones. It is striking how, in order to say something positive, the poet exploits different sensations, or organ fantasies, which are normally regarded as extremely unpleasant.

The sensation of all the tiny things in their shields, creeping and wriggling about under the skin ("shields" suggests, of course, that the poet must have insects or bugs in mind), is, after all, a sensation of terror. With artful humor, the poet entices us, through one image after the other, into accepting as positive something that would ordinarily make us shudder.

The great turnabout in the poem, where "human" and "animalistic" exchange signs with one another, spreads to all the other parts of the poem and releases entire chains of inverted images.

Sandro Key-Åberg is a poet with a considerable and warm sense of humor, to be sure, but in his poem the end result of these operations is the creation not at all of a humorous feeling but, rather, if anything, a great cosmic gravity.

He kicks the feet out from under his reader, persuades him, creates in him a fundamental uncertainty about the tenor of the poem, about whether what he is saying is serious or droll; half in jest, the reader is led into one metaphor after the other.

This method is profoundly original and has no equal anywhere in modern Swedish poetry. There is something cautious, expectant about it, a humbleness: see here! I am asking you only to make an intellectual experiment. How would it be if . . .

At the conclusion of the poem, all these amiable traps snap shut, and the reader is caught. And the poem can then fade out in a great symphonic coda of delicious originality and beauty:

> So warm the wind that blows from all the creatures!
> Together, in this wind, lives all of mankind.
>
> It is the animal that brings us together.
> It is the human that separates us.

Edith Södergran

Mitt liv, min död och mitt öde

Jag är ingenting än en omätlig vilja,
en omätlig vilja, men vartill, vartill?
Allting är mörker omkring mig,
jag kan ej lyfta ett halmstrå.
Min vilja vill blott ett, men detta ena känner
        icke jag.
När min vilja bryter fram, skall jag dö:
var hälsad mitt liv, min död och mitt öde.

1919–1920

My Life, My Death and My Fate

I am nothing but a boundless will,
a boundless will, but why, for what?
All is darkness around me.
I cannot lift a straw.
My will wants but one thing, yet this one thing I do
        not know.
When my will bursts forth, I shall die:
Hail to you, my life, my death and my fate.

1919–1920

The Enigmatic Particles in the Nucleus

With the help of a powerful magnetic field, the physicist accelerates heavy particles toward an aluminum membrane, large as a pinky fingernail and thin as a soap bubble, hung in a frame at the end of a long vacuum tube. When these particles plunge into the aluminum membrane's little galaxy, catastrophes occur. Counting tubes, calibrated for different energy levels, capture the material's silent response to the challenge. In the summary that comes out of the computer's plotter, the normal electronic droning looks like a dense rug. Out of this rug rise wavecrests of liberated energy, which say that the nucleus of the atom itself is answering the question directed to it. It is attempting to speak. Something is attempting to speak. Through the droning the depths are responding.

In this world there exists no reality. There are experimental data, and there is a horizon of concepts which attempt to interpret them. Both are variable. They collaborate with one another.

The experimental situation itself differs radically from the normal natural world.

The only things that are of the natural world in a nuclear physics laboratory are the slender crests that climb out of the background buzzing in a diagram.

There exists a profound kinship between the experimental physicist's situation and that of the poetry critic.

There is the normal linguistic background noise. There are rhythms, pulses, levels of resonance. There are well known as well as surprising sources of interference.

And then there are those singularly characteristic signals which, by their appearance, reveal that they come from greater depths, from regions in the subconscious which are even lower than those where the words are formed.

Furthest within the poem, beyond all the conventions of language and art, is a piece of independent reality which attempts to answer the reader's challenge. In this way, the enigma of a poem can coincide with a human being's enigma.

And the only reading that will be realistic is the one that is able to preserve the enigmatic element and, at the same time, isolate it from the background noise.

Edith Södergran's poem was written by a dying person. When she says she cannot lift a straw, it is not merely poetic metaphor, it is the experience of a patient suffering from high-grade tuberculosis.

When she says she is no more than a boundless will, a paradox arises which increases the poem's enormous tension; yet it is but a preparation for the still greater paradoxes which will confront us a bit further into the text.

One of the great ideational influences on the poetry of Edith Södergran was the philosopher Friedrich Nietzsche, who, like his teacher, Schopenhauer, maintained that the substance in human beings is comprised of pure will. Nietzsche's will is actually quite similar to what Sigmund Freud, some decades later, would call the libido and to what Stagnelius, in his century—and with the language of that century—called the power to desire.

The fundamental biological instability which makes us humans and facilitates our survival has many names—this strange slope, which causes us to constantly try to replace the condition we find ourselves in with another. The word "will" is actually rather abstract. It cries out for definition. In very general terms, there exists no will. Characteristic of all will is that it wants something quite definite, while fear as well as sorrow, for example, can be completely undefined emotions. How often don't we experience anguish without knowing what the anguish is all about?

But Edith Södergran's words on this boundless will which, in the midst of her weakness, she feels within her are, of course, not only a reflection of her Nietzsche studies. Rather, the fact is that Nietzsche has liberated her, given her the courage to declare, with such calm pride, that that's the way things are.

The first line of the poem is not philosophical theory, it is an empirical statement. There is something sensational, indeed harrowing, in saying something of such enormity with such calm intonation. It is precisely that kind of utterance that would normally be construed as an expression of hubris, yet it is uttered in a context that is as far removed from the regions of pride as one could possibly imagine.

And then comes the great paradox, the irregularity in a linguistic noise, which tells us that here, under this surface, is tremendous concentration; here, space is curling itself around a body of strange gravitation:

> My will wants but one thing, yet this one thing I do
> not know.

The enigmatic aspect in these lines lies neither in the individual words nor in their surrounding context. There is nothing . . . *obscure* . . . in what is being said. The enigmatic element is genuine. It is part of the very mysteriousness of human existence.

And then comes—consequently, one is tempted to say (although one doesn't know in what strange logical system such deductive rules prevail)—the conclusion:

> When my will bursts forth, I shall die:

As the result of an all too superficial reading, one could confuse this poem with a classic poetic genre: death wish poems. It does not belong there.

It is not death the poet desires. What she says is that she is entertaining a single wish which is unknown even to herself. And when it bursts forth, when it is articulated, she will die. In her wish, it is the unknown element itself that keeps her alive.

"I long for the land that does not exist," she wrote in another context.[1]

It is striking how the word "will" is consistently used in the poem, in its original, its unadulterated definition, as an expression for what *one wants oneself*. There is also a derived, or secondary, definition, where the word is frequently used as an expression for what others want one to do.

"If you only had a little more *will*, boys, you'd surely get better results at 400 meters," the physical education teacher says. What he means is: "If you wanted what I want, you would be much better boys according to my system of values," which, strictly speaking, is redundant. In this denatured version of its original definition, "will" means approximately the same as "duty" and thus, paradoxically enough, the opposite of its original meaning. To want what one actually does not want.

1. "Jag längtar till landet som icke är," from the 1925 collection *Landet som icke är* (*The Land That Does Not Exist*).

If one reads this definition into Södergran's word "will," the lines "My will wants but one thing, yet this one thing I do / not know" will be trivialized into unrecognizability. They will mean something like: I don't know what one desires of me.

It is on this point that it becomes important to know that she is a Nietzschean. With "my will" she does *not* mean "what others desire of me."

It is truly a *desire* she is speaking of. It is in this that the wonderful and the enigmatic elements of her poem consist.

Erik Blomberg

Cykladisk flöjtblåsare
(2000 år f.k.)

Hans ansikte
mot solen lyftat
likt stenen
slipad blank av havet
utan mun
utan ögon

Ljusdrucken
ur stenen stiger
dubbelflöjtens
stämma.

1943

Cycladean Flutist
(2000 B.C.)

His countenance
sunward lifted
like the stone
polished smooth by the sea
lacking mouth
lacking eyes

Giddy from the light
from the stone ascends
the voice
of the Panpipe.

1943

To Joy

Erik Blomberg was the most socially conscious of the great Swedish poets of the 1930s and 1940s. His involvement in the labor movement, like his participation in the peace movement in the 1950s, cost him much time and deprived him (of course) of the undisputed status of Official Literary Figure, which quite obviously should otherwise have been his. The position he occupies in schoolbooks and anthologies is ludicrously minor, compared with his significance as a poet, and as late as the 1960s he was still being humiliated through exclusion from a state-sponsored artistic prize, to which he was obviously entitled.

Before we approach the poem "Cycladean Flutist," we should remember that it was written by the same poet who penned the famous epitaph over the five striking sawmill workers killed by the military at Ådalen on May 14, 1931:

> Here reposes
> a Swedish worker.
> Fallen in peacetime.
> Weaponless, helpless.
> Executed
> by unknown bullets.
>
> His crime was hunger.
>
> Never forget him. [1]

As in the previously discussed poem by Tomas Tranströmer, we can see here how strong the classical Greek poetic tradition still is in our modern Swedish poetry. In the case of the Tranströmer poem, we saw how the Sapphic stanza created an impression of nature with enormous clarity and precision. In the epitaph for the fallen at Lunde,

1. Här vilar
   en svensk arbetare.
   Stupad i fredstid.
   Vapenlös, värnlös.
   Arkebuserad
   av okända kulor.

   Brottet var hunger.

   Glöm honom aldrig.

we see how the model of the laconic Greek epitaph, with the same almost enigmatic certainty, lends to troubled thoughts something of the stability of solid stone and for all time etches a great passion into the reader's reminiscences. For us, later readers, the events at Ådalen are *preserved* in this epitaph.

In principle, any poet is capable of experiencing a great, flaming passion, whether personal or, as in this case, overpersonal, but only a great poet can forge a form in which the passion remains, in which it allows itself to be preserved.

The Cyclades are an island group located in the southern part of the Aegean Sea, rich in memories from an ancient and distinctive Mediterranean culture, namely, the Aegean. One should envision the flutist sculpture spoken of in the poem "Cycladean Flutist" as one of those ancient stones shaped by time into works of art—stones that have been present in the world so long that they seem to be on their way back to their source, on their way to becoming part of nature once again. The stone has been polished smooth by the sea. The flutist no longer has a mouth, no longer has eyes. The image has ceased, in the literal sense, to represent anything at all, but adherent to it is the magic that seems to reside in the reproductive intention itself. The spoor of a human context.

On its way back into the amorphousness of nature, this stone still bears the shimmer of another world, the world of symbol, imagery, and meaning: humaniora.

Thus does man infuse the stone with meanings and fill the world with signs.

A face that no longer has a mouth cannot speak. Nor can a face that no longer has eyes see. Such a face actually has something profoundly terrifying about it. It is a picture of mutilation, of hideous transformation and lonely confinement.

In Blomberg's poem, all these frightening qualities are missing from the picture or, more correctly expressed, they are present as a shadow, a resonance, but they are not emphasized.

The idea of a human counterpart to this piece of sea-polished stone, a human flutist who has been robbed of both mouth and eyes, vibrates in close proximity to the poem without ever being allowed to enter into it.

But this undertone remains throughout the entire poem.

Man fills the stone, the dead material, with content, with significance. And then the miracle occurs: these significations return.

Out of Blomberg's maltreated, archaic stone sculpture there arises, after millennia, the voice of the flute. Pan's instrument, the instrument of ancient rite.

Swedish lyric poetry more often expresses sorrow than happiness. A surprising amount of it—after the Period of Great Power—deals with passivity, ranging all the way from the surrendering of all desires to the more sophisticated adaptation to what is feasible. Occasionally, it can appear as if, during the course of entire epochs, poetry were the only sector of the language where Sweden, historical Sweden, has placed all its dejection, all its submissiveness. The compulsion to renounce strongly dominates over the power to desire. The aesthetic intoxication of a Petrarch, the shimmer of light surrounding Cavalcanti's "Donna me pregha," Leopardi's bold hunger for life, the glistening of crystal, the bouquet of wine, the sensation of living skin under gleaming silk—in short, the power to desire—are basically alien to this poetic tradition. The Swedish tradition stands much closer to Hölderlin's lament:

> Woe is me. Where, when it is winter,
> Do I take the flowers, and where
> The sunshine
> And shadows of the earth?
> The walls stand
> Speechless and cold. In the wind
> The weather vanes clatter.[2]

In the Swedish tradition, mixed with this approaching winter chill, there is frequently something which, with certain justification, could be called a sharecropper motif, an obsequious bowing with cap in hand as one stands at the door:

2. Weh mir, wo nehm ich, wenn   Sprachlos und kalt, im Winde
   Es Winter ist, die Blumen, und wo   Klirren die Fahnen.
   Den Sonnenschein
   Und Schatten der Erde?
   Die Mauern stehn

I do not wish to look behind
nor forward for some time yet,
all is vigil and of the mind
and life and death my friends well met.

Pär Lagerkvist[3]

or,

On an early summer day the clover blossoms
silently receive the bumblebees at a farewell party.
It is done with dignity
and the bumblebee gives thanks for all that has been.

Harry Martinson[4]

or,

I heard how the barley was cut by the scythe,
as the leaves and the waters were roaring;
now with its flail comes the harvest of my heart,
now quiet must I be, like the grove.

P. D. A. Atterbom[5]

All this, particularly the last example, is good poetry. The scale

3. Ej skall jag se tillbaka
   ej heller framåt än,
   allt minne är och vaka
   och liv och död min vän.
4. I försommardagen ta klöverblommorna
   tyst emot humlorna på en avskedsbjudning.
   Det sker värdigt
   och humlan tackar för allt som har varit.
5. Jag hörde hur kornet av lian skars,
   då brusade löven och sunden;
   nu kommer med slagan mitt hjärtas höst,
   och nu må jag tiga, som lunden.

ranges from good to very good, I would say, but the thing that is so striking in all the quotations is that silence and resignation are represented, so self-evidently, as the solution to the respective situations—as if a human voice has never been raised against death, or as if no one has ever overturned a backgammon board in a moment of anger and said: "No, gentlemen, I refuse to play this game!"

It goes without saying that literature is part of social life, inasmuch as it belongs to those symbolic constructions by means of which man attempts to give significance to his life and, above all, to fit his suffering into a rational context. It is precisely for this reason that the tradition appears adventurous.

It possesses dominance, but it is not entirely dominant. In the self-confident, jubilant hymns of Wallin's *Hymnbook* (*1819 Års Psalmbok*) —for example, Samuel Hedborn's "Nu segrar alla trognas hopp" ("Victorious Now the Hopes of All the Faithful")—it is not to be found. In the works of Bellman, it is driven away with a bitter grimace, a strumming of the lute, the slap of a playing card on the table— but bitterly, oh so bitterly, so desperately. In the poets of the Period of Great Power—who can be profoundly melancholy, melancholy unto death (but that is another matter)—this attitude has not yet evolved. Between Bo Bergman's debut (1903) and that of Karl Asplund (1912), it is not possible to open a book of poetry which, on every other page, does not maintain that it is our obligation to submit to our fate, and for some time *this* attitude becomes, for the Swedish poetry-reading public, almost identical to a *poetic* attitude toward life in general.

It is against that background that one must view the refreshing and, of course, provocative aspects in the conduct of the Fem Unga (Five Young Men).[6] Artur Lundkvist's greatest significance at that moment had to have consisted in the fact that he showed us the image of a poet who considers it completely compatible with a poetic attitude to *desire* something of life—this at a time when poetic *finesse*, for all practical purposes, consisted of behaving like an unmarried

6. Artur Lundkvist, Harry Martinson, Erik Asklund, Josef Kjellgren, and Gustav Sandgren were named the Five Young Men after the appearance of their *5 unga* (1929), an anthology of experimental modernistic poetry which heralded the breakthrough of vitalist, surrealist-inspired poetry in Sweden.

schoolmarm at a church tea when the cookie tray comes around for the second time: "Goodness gracious, no!"

> I want to shout out the joy of life and laugh
>   with a strong jaw.
> I want to stagger, soused, drunk on the superfluity
>   of life's joy.
> I want to sing sublime songs in times when the harvest
>   is good and hearts are overfull.

Artur Lundkvist [7]

If you place such a stanza in the hands of a student in the year 1975, when these notes are being written, there is a considerable risk that he or she will see only a large and robust man, who is saying that it is pleasant to get drunk and bellow a song. Because the student of 1975 has had far too limited an experience with the propaganda of humility being conducted within such great expanses of Swedish poetry, even when that poetry is good to very good. And it is against this that the young Lundkvist is speaking out.

The flute note that climbs out of the ancient Cycladean stone in Erik Blomberg's poem is an unmistakably triumphant note. An ecstasy that has survived time, silence, blindness, and disintegration, a clear and piercing note from within the stone, from within the depths of history.

The person who is perceptive enough to listen to this inaudible, yet sharp, flute melody from a piece of decaying stone must of necessity also perceive why those striking, impoverished sawmill workers from the northern Swedish province of Norrland would rather defy Captain Mesterton's machine gun–toting patrols than allow themselves to be debased by foreign strikebreakers.

7. Jag vill skrika ut livets fröjd och skratta
    med en stark käft.
  Jag vill ragla rusig, drucken av livsfröjdens
    överflöd.
  Jag vill sjunga höga visor i tider då skörden
    är god och hjärtana överfulla.

From the depths of this stone arises a pure, deeply amoral joy, a joy associated with the existence of history itself, of civilization.

The posture of the little flutist, who is being weathered away from the ancient stone, is the posture of one who is in the midst of a kind of intoxication, or a feeling of profound joy.

> His countenance
> sunward lifted

Thus the stone surrounding the flutist will weather away, and only his flute tone will remain.

With this poem Blomberg establishes a connection with the larger design, with the immense electrical network of world poetry. With the traditions of joy.